D0924822

GAWAIN AND THE GREEN KNIGHT

Also by Nicholas Stuart Gray

Plays

BEAUTY AND THE BEAST
THE TINDER BOX
THE HUNTERS AND THE HENWIFE
THE PRINCESS AND THE SWINEHERD
THE MARVELLOUS STORY OF PUSS IN BOOTS
NEW CLOTHES FOR THE EMPEROR
THE IMPERIAL NIGHTINGALE
THE OTHER CINDERELLA
THE SEVENTH SWAN
THE WRONG SIDE OF THE MOON (THE STONE CAGE)
NEW LAMPS FOR OLD
GAWAIN AND THE GREEN KNIGHT

Fiction

OVER THE HILLS TO FABYLON
DOWN IN THE CELLAR
THE SEVENTH SWAN
THE STONE CAGE
THE APPLE-STONE
GRIMBOLD'S OTHER WORLD
MAINLY IN THE MOONLIGHT

Biography

THE BOYS

GAWAIN
AND THE
GREEN KNIGHT

A Play by

NICHOLAS STUART GRAY

Illustrated by Victor Ambrus

London

DENNIS DOBSON

First published in Great Britain in 1969 by
Dobson Books Ltd., 80 Kensington Church Street, London W.8.
Printed by St. Stephen's Bristol Press Ltd., Bristol.
Bound edition SBN 234 77976 4
Paper edition SBN 234 77099 6

TO VAL AND ADRIAN,

slainte mhath!

CHARACTERS

[In order of appearance]

SIR KAY

THE KING

THE QUEEN

HIS SQUIRE

GAWAIN

THE GREEN KNIGHT*

THE LADY RAGNELL

THE LADY MIRIEL

SIR BERCILAK*

* This is the same character, though it should look on the programme as if one actor is playing two parts, thus trying to save the denoument for its place in the play.

The play is based on the marvellous Middle English poem, and on the ancient legend of the Loathly Lady.

ACT ONE

Scene 1: The parlour at Narberth Castle in North Wales.
Scene 2: The same, two days later.

ACT TWO

Scene: A room in a Northumberland castle.

ACT THREE

Scene 1: A mountain-side at midnight.
Scene 2: The Queen's dressing-room at Narberth.
Scene 3: The parlour at Narberth Castle. The same evening.

PERIOD

An intermingling of A.D. 500 and A.D. 1200. Malory did it, too, so see if I care.

THE PARLOUR AT NARBERTH CASTLE IN
NORTH WALES

Down left and right are large square windows in stone frames, closed against the winter. Through their horn covering, snow can be seen falling. There is a huge fireplace up right, in which logs are burning. At the back is a door, also closed. Tapestries are hung about the rough stone walls, and unlit torches stand in brackets here and there. A great sword is set in a shallow niche in one wall. By the fireside stand stools, and a chair. Over on the left are other stools, round a table. The room is not square, but part of an octagonal, for it is in the side-tower of the main keep. It has been decorated with holly and mistletoe. It is afternoon, and the light will soon be going.

The KING *is playing chess with* SIR KAY, *at the table. The*

*former is the handsome wreck of a once-superb athlete.
Not burly, but wide-shouldered and indomitable. Because
of old wounds, and recent illness, he moves stiffly, and
with a noticeable limp. His fair hair is going grey, so is
his short beard, and down one cheek runs an old scar. He
is about forty-five. An habitual watcher of other people,
from a sincere wish to understand and like them. When he
speaks, his voice is deep and gentle; but he has a strong
sense of humour that occasionally betrays him into an in-
ability to speak at all, or only weakly. When needed, his
authority is absolute, and he could be physically
formidable if roused. He always has a good deal on his
mind. He is simply dressed in a pleated, calf-length tunic
of plain wool, and he wears thick woollen stockings. He
prefers to be thought simple.*

KAY *is five years his elder. He is dark, tall, thin and
muscular. A quick-moving, edgy man. Fundamentally
kind, he tries to conceal the fact behind a scathing tongue.
Those who know him pay little attention to his bark,
though anyone would be wise to avoid his bite. He is
managerial, and is irritated past bearing if anything gets
beyond his control. His loyalty to the* KING *is un-
swerving. He admires, loves, and bullies him.*

The KING *is looking at the chess-board, and* KAY *is looking at the* KING. *After a few moments,* KAY'S *fingers start
to tap impatiently on the table-top.*

KAY. You must make *some* sort of move! We can't sit
here forever, just aging.

KING. Very well. I'll castle the king.

> [*He moves two of his men, to accomplish this.*
> KAY *groans.*]

You don't like that?

KAY. Bruno, if you play your men to please me, this is not chess as I was taught. You can't be serious. Take it back. I'll shut my eyes, and pretend not to notice.

KING. Very kind. And cheating, as *I* was taught. I see no reason, anyway, to change the move. The king stays castled.

KAY. If you made war as you play chess, all Britain would now be a Saxon settlement. You and I, dear brother, would be slaves—or dead.

KING. What about making your own move, instead of nagging and aging?

KAY. You've asked for it.

> [*He moves a man.*]

Check!

KING. Very clever. But the king's knight intercepts.

> [*He also moves a man.*]

KAY. You'll lose him, you know. You can't afford that. Where are you going?

> [*The* KING *has risen abruptly, and gone limping to the window.*]

It's no use jumping up and down all the time!

KING. I can't afford to lose a knight—or a single pawn——

KAY. Nor to bring on another fever, worrying. There will be a messenger, Bruno. It's no good staring down an empty road every five minutes. It won't bring him any the faster. Just forget about it.

KING. Don't be ridiculous! It must be over now. By at least a week. Was there anyone left to bring a message?

KAY. If not, you'd hear from other sources. I tell you, the snow has delayed the journey. It's a strange time of year for the Saxons to start trouble, anyway. Communications are almost impossible. But someone will get through.

KING. I should have been there.

KAY. They'd enough on their hands without nursing you. You can't even sit a horse, let alone fight a battle. Look, I don't like sitting here in safety, any more than you do. *My* men are fighting——

KING. Your choice, Kay.

KAY. And a hard one. But my choice, and that of all your war-leaders. Your recovery is more important to Britain than one small battle, even with *your* sword. For all our sakes—Bruno—come and sit down.

> [*The* KING *slowly comes back to the table and sits.*]

KING. Where had we got to?

KAY. You'd just made a lunatic move that put your knight in hazard. He's going to fall to my castle.

> [*He moves a man, and the* KING *then moves one of his.*]

KING. The queen protects him.

KAY. Yes, well—you'll lose her to my bishop, and that will be checkmate to your king.

KING. How brutal you are, Kay.

KAY. I didn't invent the rules. Just because you can't play chess——

> [*The door opens, and the* QUEEN *enters. She carries a tray with food on it. She is a beautiful woman of about thirty-four. Her hair is the colour of dark honey, bound high about her head, though she wears no crown. She is dressed nearly as simply as the* KING, *in a blue gown with an apron over it. She is a wise and generous person, and usually her manner is relaxed and charming. If forced to be formal, she can seem cold and aloof, but this is not her true nature.*]

She can also be somewhat bossy at times. To the best of her ability she tries to protect the KING *from such threats to his peace of mind as she sees coming. There is something below the surface of her relationship with him that holds a seed of trouble. She sets her tray on a stool, and glances smilingly at the two men.*]

KING. Vera, there's an awful bishop threatening my queen, and my knight is about to be collared by a castle, and I'm going to lose the game.

QUEEN. [*Lightly*] Alas for you!

KING. So, to save them—I surrender.

QUEEN. Most chivalrous.

KAY. Not at all. He's in the soup, anyway.

KING [*Going to the window*] Luckily, in a game, one can always surrender.

KAY. I'll save you the disgrace.

[*He tips over the board, scattering the chessmen.*]

QUEEN. Now they're all lost.

KING [*Unheeding all this*]. Will no one ever come?

KAY [*To* QUEEN]. What have you got there?

QUEEN. Bread and honey. I thought we could all get sticky together by the fire.

KAY. Did *you* have to carry it! Where are the servants?

QUEEN. Out skating. Except the very ancient, who are much too creaky to totter up here.

KAY. Skating! It'll be dark soon.

QUEEN. They have torches.

KAY [*Sourly*]. I hope they melt the ice with them and drown! They should have asked me, before leaving the castle empty. I'm the seneschal——

QUEEN. Dear Kay, they had *my* leave. Scold *me*.

[13]

KAY. You, madam, are above reproach.

QUEEN. How very nice.

> [KAY *makes a helpless gesture towards the* KING. *She nods.*]

Bruno, come over to the fire, dear.

> [*As he does not move, she goes to him, and touches his arm.*]

There's a frightful draught from that window, and it's time for your medicine, anyway.

> [*He looks at her at last, and makes a wry face.*]

KAY. Hence the honey. To take away the nasty taste.

KING. It would be better employed sweetening your tongue.

KAY. I've had it fifty years. To change it, you must cut it off.

KING. We wouldn't recognise you. Go on being the spiteful monster we know and love. Vera, has no message come at all?

> [*The* QUEEN *has poured some syrup from a flagon into a spoon.*]

I don't *need* this stuff any longer. I'm perfectly well.

KAY. Do what your kind wife says.

KING. You're joining forces. It's probably treason! Vera, hasn't anyone——?

QUEEN. If you take this, I'll tell you.

> [*He gulps down the syrup eagerly. She pours honey into the spoon.*]

KING. There *has* been a message!

> [*She holds out the spoon in silence. He swallows the honey.*]

Please!

QUEEN. Yes. A man rode in with word from Bors——

KAY. What's he doing?

QUEEN. Bors?

KAY. No, no! The man—the messenger!

QUEEN. Drinking some soup that I hotted. He's exhausted.
He needs sleep——

KAY. He won't shut one eye till I have his message. Or
did he tell you? *I* am the proper person to bring word
to the king.

KING [*Forcefully*]. Kay, go and bring his news at once.
And hurry!

KAY. We may be informal here, but——

> [*He catches the* KING'S *eye, and goes off briskly,
> centre.*]

KING. But one breath from outside, and back comes
ceremony. You *were* given the message, weren't you?

QUEEN. Let Kay tell you.

KING. Do you want to see me go mad?

QUEEN. The Saxons are dispersed. Now sit down.

KING. What about——?

QUEEN. Our men have only minor injuries. Please sit
down, Bruno.

> [*He gives a great sigh, and sits in the chair by
> the fire.*]

Now don't let poor Kay know I told you.

KING. He gets so irritated by trifles. I must have another
little talk with him.

QUEEN. You and your little talks with everyone! What do
you think these little talks do?

KING. They go in at one ear and out of the other. I know.
But I always hope a word will stick occasionally. And
hope is cheap, they say.

> [*A log falls out on the hearth, and she kneels to
> replace it.*]

Let me do that. You'll get filthy. Now look at you!

QUEEN. A smudge. You know, there was a time—and we're *not* old, Bruno!—when you were just the war-chief, and I the girl you married for her dowry of a hundred fighting men——

KING. Marriage was discussed before the dowry. Don't put it like that.

QUEEN. When I went campaigning with you. When we were snow-bound, or beseiged in the little hill-forts—and I did far more than mend fires or carry trays. No one stopped me from helping the doctors—using a knife in surgery myself—and brewing herbs for medicines, like the one that has cured your fever——

KING. Witchcraft! You be careful. That reputation tends to cling. You wouldn't like being burnt in a market-place. And I wouldn't like to watch.

QUEEN [*Amused*]. Would you merely watch?

KING. I might applaud, if you were very brave—as you would be. [*He shivers*] It's cold in here.

QUEEN. Put this round you.

> [*She brings a cloak to drape about his shoulders, as* KAY *enters.*]

KAY. The man has made his report. Though no one had time, apparently, to set it properly in writing——

KING. Get on with it, Kay.

KAY. The sea-raid is beaten off. Survivors took to their ships. Only ten of our men hurt—including Bors—none severely. He reckons the pirates will try to make a landing further North, but there are so few that it won't be hard to stop them. Look.

> [*He pulls aside a tapestry left of the door, and shows a map fastened to the wall behind. The map is large and shaped roughly like Britain, though far from accurate here and there in out-*

[16]

*line. It is coloured green, which varies in shade
—almost yellow in the more civilised areas, and
something near black in the outer reaches.
Dotted about it are small, lance-shaped stickers,
each carrying a bright pennant.* KAY *takes one
of the stickers from the East coast*]

Bors is moving his troop to intercept—up here.

    [*He places the sticker higher on the coastline.*]

KING. I knew he'd do it! He's a fine leader.

KAY. Deputy leader. They will have missed you there.

KING. Ah, they don't need me any more.

QUEEN. What nonsense! Your battle is for health at the
moment. If anything happened to you, there would be
no troops—no Britain! Your men fight only for you.
And, there's your sword—but it goes with them into
every skirmish, and they know it. It's their symbol of
victory. Now have some bread and butter.

    [*She sits down, and begins busily to butter
some bread.*]

KING. Yes—yes. It will be months before the Saxons can
mount another raid in force. We'll stop worrying, and
concentrate on Christmas.

QUEEN [*Gaily*]. And let me look after you both, as though
we were back in the past of our youth. I'll do some
cooking. It won't be hard to minister to a family of
three.

KING. Four.

QUEEN. What, dear?

KING. Four. I've sent for Gawain.

    [*A slight pause.*]

QUEEN. Oh, no!

KAY. Are you mad!

QUEEN. You haven't really?

[17]

KING. Why not? He is my nephew. Part of the family, surely? We haven't seen him for far too long.

KAY. Not long enough for me!

QUEEN. Oh, but our peaceful retreat here——!

KING. I want him to be part of it.

KAY. If you contemplate any peace with that maniac about——!

QUEEN. Think of the last time he came. To our wedding. It was chaos!

KING. Now, now! That was fifteen years ago. He had a run of bad luck, poor boy, and he so newly knighted.

QUEEN. *He* had bad luck! What about that woman he beheaded?

KING. Quite unintentionally. He was aiming at her husband.

KAY. *After* the fellow had surrendered. A knightly aim!

KING. The fellow had killed two of Gawain's loved hounds, right under his nose. The boy lost his temper. Then the man's wife ran between them and—well, it was an accident. He said he shut his eyes as he struck.

QUEEN. If Gawain can't look what he's doing, he shouldn't be trusted with a sharp instrument!

KING [*Trying not to laugh*]. Bit impulsive.

KAY. I also remember a most unseemly episode with the lady-love of Sir Pelleas. Do you excuse that?

KING. No, no. Most unfortunate.

QUEEN. Had his eyes shut, I suppose.

KING. I wouldn't put it past him.

QUEEN. It's nothing to laugh at.

KING. No, dear, no. But—he was only nineteen. And it did rather show up the Lady Ettard. Sir Pelleas found a much nicer one as a result——

QUEEN. Are you suggesting it was all a brilliant plot, on

[18]

the part of your dear nephew, to disentangle Sir Pelleas?

KING. Did anyone ask my dear nephew? The world sprang happily with its claws out, to brand him false and wanton. He may easily have planned the whole thing, not wisely but with good intent.

KAY. What stopped him saying so, then?

KING. Oh, pride. He was judged unheard, so he wouldn't plead. Mind you, I'm only guessing. But I always wondered——

KAY. Pelleas didn't. Only your command prevented murder. And he walloped Gawain all over the tilt-yard whenever they met, until he tucked in his tail and fled home to Mum.

QUEEN. On that subject, you spoke of witchcraft a little earlier——

KING. Now, now! My half-sister has her faults, as we know, but——

KAY. She's a monster, *that* we know! She'll never forgive you for forcing this uneasy truce on Scotland. She only married into Scotland to have the right to be your enemy.

KING. The more reason for me to have the handling of her sons.

QUEEN. But not *now* while you need quiet. Don't let Gawain come here.

KING. I sent for him months back. He should be here already. To spend the Yuletide festival——

KAY. Yuletide? What would that mean to him? The pagan rites of the wild North—and his own mother the High Priestess.

KING. Kay, he is heir to Britain. What sort of king will he make, if he never leaves his wild North?

KAY. It's a good question, wherever he is!

KING. Do give him a chance. He'll have changed with the passing years.

KAY. Wait another fifty!

QUEEN [*Hopefully*]. Perhaps he won't come. She keeps her sons in a grip of iron. She'll never let him go.

KING. She'll never pass over the chance of ruling Britain one day, through him. I wrote saying I'd call a council and elect another heir, unless she hands him over now. Like it or leave it, my dears, he will come. And I can't think what's delaying him.

> [KAY *crosses to the map on the wall, and surveys it gloomily.*]

KAY. It always made me feel secure, to see the lances and pennants of your men—here, and here—and here. Bors at Loidis now. Ours at Narberth. And the white falcon of Gawain, well out of everyone's way—right up *there!*

> [*He has been indicating various places on the map, and now he points to the most northerly and blackest part of it.*]

KING. Oh, come on, you two! Be charitable. The years will have steadied him. There'll be no sort of rumpus—

> [*From outside the window, left, comes a sudden skirl of nearing pipe-music. A shout, and other shouts in reply. Those in the room look at one another. The skirling dies out in a long screech. KAY takes the pennant from Orkney and sticks it savagely among those of Narberth.*]

KAY. That's it, then!

QUEEN [*To* KING]. I hope your nerves will stand this.

KING. So do I. You'd better go down, Kay.

KAY. I'm just collecting my strength.

*[He goes towards the door. But it flies open, and
the* SQUIRE *is standing there, lifting one arm in
flamboyant greeting. He is a tall, sturdy fellow
of thirty-three. He wears a helmet, and a sur-
coat with a white falcon blazoned on it. His tunic
and leggings are of bright, red-checked cloth. He
also wears, on a normally strong and pleasant
face, a look of grim determination. He has carefully rehearsed this performance. He removes
his helmet, revealing red hair. A practical,
sensible, reliable person, he has also a fiercely
protective streak, of which the main object is
always* GAWAIN, *whom he tends to regard as his
life's work.* KAY *stares at him bleakly.]*

If you're Gawain, you *have* changed!

SQUIRE. Well, I'm not. I'm his squire.

*[His voice has a slight Highland lilt. Caught off
balance for a moment, he recovers, and goes on
in ringing tones:]*

I announce the arrival of the High Prince of Orkney
and Lothian—son of King Loth—son of the Queen
Morgan-Morgawse—nephew of the dreaded and mighty
king of Britain——

KING. Er—we're quite informal here, my dear boy.

QUEEN [*Crossly*]. We're not dressed for this sort of thing!

SQUIRE [*At the top of his voice*]. Gawain of Orkney!

[He stands aside. GAWAIN *strides into the room,
checks, and halts. This gives the impression of
a bull entering a china-shop and wondering
where to begin.* KAY *groans softly.* GAWAIN *is not
as tall as the* SQUIRE, *but as strongly-built and
faster-moving. He wears a metal helmet over a
hood of chain-mail, a tunic of red-checked wool,*

*with mailed sleeves. His leggings are red leather,
so is the belt that carries his sword. Over one
shoulder is draped a long plaid of the same red
material as the tunic. His shield is painted with
a white falcon. He has a close-cut, red-gold
beard. He seems to blaze in the quiet room. He
could scarcely be more out of place there if he
tried. And he is trying hard. The bright impact
of the men from the Orkneys blinds the on-
lookers temporarily to the fact that they are the
worse for wear, and their clothing a bit shabby
and thread-bare.*

GAWAIN'S *main difficulty in life is his endless war
with himself. He can only relax when faced with
something simple—like a three-headed dragon
(but these are thin on the ground). His terrible
mother has so sapped his confidence that he is
always vulnerable. Too proud to endure criticism,
and too unaccustomed to praise to believe it. He
does not like himself, and is unwilling to risk
liking others. He thinks no one else could like
him, and thinks he does not care. His theories
about life frequently trip him into falling flat
on his face. He is about to embark on a hopeless
battle with his own defences, not to fall deeply
in love with his uncle, his aunt, and anyone else
who throws him a kind word. He speaks with
the same lilt as his* SQUIRE.]

GAWAIN [*Just to be awkward*]. Which is the king?

KING. Now, now, Gawain. You've not forgotten me. Nor I
you.

[GAWAIN *tosses his shield to the* SQUIRE, *goes to
the* KING, *and drops formally to one knee.*]

[22]

GAWAIN. My dread lord. My good uncle. Great King Arthur.

> [*He kisses the* KING'S *hand, before the* KING *can prevent him.*]

KAY. I knew it would be like this!

KING. Yes—well, do get up. I'm delighted to see you. Oh, get up, Gawain.

> [*He pulls him to his feet, removes his helmet neatly, and hands it to* KAY, *then pushes back the mailed hood till it lies on his nephew's shoulders, revealing his bright hair, and kisses him on both cheeks. After which, he holds him at arms'-length and inspects him.*]

No, you haven't changed at all.

GAWAIN. Should I apologise, sir?

KING [*Amused*]. Oh, not yet. Now, I'm sure you remember the Queen?

GAWAIN. Forgive me, madam. You were in the shadows.

> [*He goes to her. She, hypnotised by all this grandeur, affects an over-regal attitude. Smiling tightly, she extends a hand to be formally kissed.* GAWAIN *pauses long enough to show everyone that he knows what is expected, then——*]

[*Cheerfully*] Auntie Vera!

> [*He kisses her heartily on both cheeks. For an instant, one wicked gleam crosses his face at her expression. The* KING *glances at* KAY, *who lifts his eyes to heaven.* GAWAIN *catches this last bit, and starts on* KAY.]

And our retainers must meet each other. This is my squire, Torcull.

KAY [*Angrily*]. I am not a retainer!

KING [*Hurriedly*]. Sir Kay, my foster-brother. You have met, you know.

GAWAIN [*In mock surprise*]. The years have altered you, sir.

KAY [*Sourly*]. Not you, sir.

GAWAIN. I fear you flatter, sir.

> [*He abandons* KAY *with a careless bow, and turns to the* KING *and* QUEEN.]

My mother, the High Queen, sends sisterly greeting to you, my lord. And to you, lady—I feel sure.

QUEEN [*Tartly*]. Most kind.

> [GAWAIN *peels off his mailed gloves, and throws them to his* SQUIRE, *who is taken by surprise, and drops them with a clatter.*]

KING. Now isn't this all splendid? So much to talk about. My dear Gawain, I hope you'll soon feel at home with us—your own family——

KAY. I'm no relative, I'm happy to——

KING. Er—Kay, will you go, very kindly, and arrange about quarters? Proper and fitting quarters for Gawain and——

KAY [*Muttering*]. There's a good dungeon——

KING. Kay, please!

> [KAY *sniffs. He then catches the* KING'S *eye. He takes a deep breath, and turns more graciously to* GAWAIN. *He speaks quite sincerely, needing the information he asks.*]

How many of your warriors and retainers must be housed?

GAWAIN [*With a snap*]. One. My squire.

KAY. Oh. The High Prince of Orkney and Lothian travels lightly.

> [*He cannot resist the opening, and the* KING'S

sound of protest comes too late].

GAWAIN [*Balefully*]. Your land is too tame for me to need soldiers. As you would know, if you ever ventured beyond these strong stone walls.

SQUIRE. Orkney himself can guard himself from any attack—or affront!

KING. All right, you two. Kay meant no affront. He was joking.

GAWAIN [*To* KAY]. Forgive me, sir. I come from a land of fighters, and forget sometimes to make allowance for the aged and retired.

> [*The* KING *takes charge of the situation, with quiet authority.*]

KING. Gawain, you will please stop goading Sir Kay. Come here. Instantly.

GAWAIN [*Obeying*]. Dread my lord.

KING. And stop saying that. If you drive me into deserving the adjective, it will spoil Christmas for you.

KAY [*Under his breath*]. *Make* Christmas for *me!*

KING. Kay.

KAY. I'm going.

> [*He starts to go, catches the* KING'S *eye, turns, and says rather sweetly:*]

I'm glad you're here, Sir Gawain.

GAWAIN [*Responding at once*]. You disarm me, sir.

KAY. Not before time, sir.

> [*He goes off, with the honours of war. The* KING *is quick to build on this.*]

KING. Yes—take off your sword, Gawain. No need for it among friends. Come to the fire. Here—Torcull——

> [*He removes* GAWAIN'S *sword, and hands it to the* SQUIRE, *who puts it with the other armour. Having been disarmed, in several senses,*

GAWAIN *now simmers down considerably, and with some relief to himself.*]

Tell me, now, when did you leave Scotland?

GAWAIN. When my lady mother—when I had your command, sir. Three months ago.

KING. She—er—she made no difficulties?

GAWAIN [*Suddenly grinning*]. Not when she'd thought it over.

[*But he sobers, too quickly.*]

She said you—your court must be growing old, to become so lenient.

KING. Did she, indeed? My kind sister is mistaken. I became impatient. I'd hoped to see you before now.

GAWAIN. You could have sent—if you'd wanted me.

KING. Gawain, I've written to you at least twice a year for fifteen years! And sent verbal messages. *All* wanting you.

GAWAIN. They never reached me.

SQUIRE. She stopped them! She burnt the letters. She silenced the messengers, the High Queen!

GAWAIN. Keep your mouth shut! [*To the* KING]. My mother cannot have realised you truly meant——

KING [*Dryly*]. Until I made my wishes a command. Did she tell you I'd disinherit you, unless you came?

GAWAIN. No. Just the bit about you growing old.

KING. Dear Morgan-Morgawse! Let's talk of gentler things. Did you meet any dragons or ogres on your journey?

GAWAIN [*Not sure how to take this*]. Well—there were some obstacles on the road, sir. The Lowlands of my country are not over-fond of my race. There were other wolves, also. Some Saxon war-bands, raiding inland, we helped with those.

[26]

SQUIRE. And that daft Sir Bruce! Three weeks in his horrible wet cellar! And we in chains. All those rats. If his daughter hadn't taken pity——

GAWAIN. Mallachd ort! [*Mollach orsht*] *Will* you keep——!

> [*The* SQUIRE *subsides.* GAWAIN *gives a small cough, and says sedately:*]

Och, we managed.

KING [*Weakly*]. Well done.

> [*The* QUEEN *gives the smallest squeak of laughter.* GAWAIN *stiffens. The* KING *looks from him to the* QUEEN *and back. His tone changes*].

I'm a terrible host to you, Gawain. You must be starving. And weary to the bone. Torcull, too. I've offered not even a cup of wine in welcome. Now, look, there's some bread and honey—oh, that's not enough. Guinevere——

QUEEN. I'll send some proper food, to stay the pangs till supper.

> [GAWAIN *and his* SQUIRE *bow to her, as she goes out centre.*]

KING. Now then, sit down, Gawain.

GAWAIN. Not in your presence, my dr—my loved lord.

KING [*Patiently*]. It's an order, Gawain.

> [*His nephew sits on a stool by the fire.*]

Thank you, Gawain.

GAWAIN [*Plaintively*]. I'm not quite meaning to be difficult.

KING. Really? Well—just get it right into your head that you're my dear nephew, and relax, and give us a chance to know you. Is that so hard to do?

GAWAIN. People have awful long memories. Old tales die hard.

KING. If you don't bother to contradict them.

GAWAIN [*Surprised*]. Sir?

KING. Trail your cloak in the dust and plenty will step on it. A thrown glove will be snatched up—as you found with Kay, just now.

GAWAIN. He started it.

KING. He did not. And I want a little talk with you about him. Kay's a very kind, good man. You must get used to his tongue. His actions speak differently. Also, he is sixteen years your senior, and entitled to respect.

GAWAIN. Was I discourteous, sir?

KING. You are always courteous in words. It's one of your great charms, as I remember. And often extremely aggravating! No, don't argue. I've been fairly ill, as your mother may have told you, and I need quiet to recover. Help me, Gawain, for pity's sake.

> [*The* KING *is now sitting in the chair by the fire, and* GAWAIN *drops to his knees at his side.*]

GAWAIN. I am at your command, sir.

KING. That's good. Then we can make some plans. First, a good meal for you, and a rest. Then you can ride into the town with Kay, and be introduced to some local worthies. Scatter largesse among the lesser fry, and——

> [GAWAIN *has started, and the* SQUIRE *makes an abrupt movement. The* KING *looks at them.*]

You won't mind that? They're very friendly in this place.

> [*He stops again, and has another good look at his nephew. Then he runs a hand along his shoulder.*]

[28]

Man, you're soaking wet! I hadn't noticed the snow melting on you. Well, I'm a fool, and a poor host again. You must get into dry clothes, both of you, or *you'll* be down with fever next. Torcull, did you arrange for the unloading of your pack-horses?

SQUIRE [*Blankly*]. Pack-horses?

GAWAIN. We've none. We brought only what's on our own backs, and those of the two war-horses. We—came lightly. For greater speed.

KING. I see. In that case, come with me, and my wardrobe will supply—

[*He has risen. And* GAWAIN *rises also.*]

No, wait. The Queen is sending food up here. You'd better stay by the fire. Er—Torcull, you come, I'll give you some——

[*The others move closer together. The* KING *surveys them, and smiles kindly.*]

No, of course you don't want to be separated, in a strange household, the moment you arrive. Stay together, then. I'll find one of the pages. Try to get warm, the pair of you, and I won't be long.

[*He goes out. A pause.* GAWAIN *sits by the fire again. The* SQUIRE *moves to his side, and he gives an abrupt sigh, and leans his head against the other.*]

GAWAIN. I wish I was home again.

SQUIRE. You'll stay here, in your proper place, and no nonsense.

GAWAIN. I can't keep it up, Gaheris.

GAHERIS [*As this is his right name*]. You're doing fine. You stood up to them.

[29]

GAWAIN. Och, I'd be glad for them to find another for their crown! You—or Gareth, forbye.

GAHERIS. I can see mother standing for that! And she knowing too well that she hasn't the hold on me that she's got on you. She fair tore you apart when you ran home the last time!

GAWAIN. They'll tear me here, let me make one false move.

GAHERIS. The king likes you.

GAWAIN. He had me weighed. I'm going back.

[*He has risen, and now moves towards the door.* GAHERIS *catches him.*]

GAHERIS. Don't be a fool, Gawain! She'll pack you straight back here. With a rap on the knuckles to leave them raw! Oh, the good gods, Gawain! Look how she sent you on this journey—all alone, as though you'd been a ghillie! If I had not slid down the wall, and followed you—ach, mo chridhe! [*mo chree*] The Prince of Scotland, who should have led a grand tail of warriors— with the standards flying, and the pipes skirling to the skies———!

GAWAIN. You did all right, with the pennant, and the bit piping.

GAHERIS. It was not enough!

GAWAIN. No matter. We've other troubles on us now. How much money have we got?

GAHERIS. Awful little.

GAWAIN. Let's have a look. You heard what he said about largesse?

[*They empty their wallets on the table. There are very few coins to show.*]

Just what did he mean by "scattering"?

GAHERIS. This lot won't scatter far!

GAWAIN. Gaheris, what shall we do? We cannot admit how poor we are. It was bad enough about the pack-horses——

> [*The* QUEEN *enters. She is about to call in some-one outside, with food, but sees the brothers counting their coins. She halts the unseen servant.*]

GAHERIS. There's that gambling game I can play. With the coin and the three cups. I could get with the other squires and things, and win us some money, Gawain.

GAWAIN. Aye, that's an idea. But no cheating, the way you do with us at home.

GAHERIS [*Shocked*]. That's different, in the family.

QUEEN [*To servant outside*]. Let me take that.

> [*The brothers start and turn. The* QUEEN *brings a loaded tray down to the fire. Her formal manner is now abandoned, and she is easy and kind with the Orkneys.*]

If you two will clear that stool for me——

> [*The brothers hurry to help her. She pours a cup of wine.*]

Gawain.

> [*She hands it to him, and pours another and gives it to* GAHERIS.]

And—Gaheris, is it? Or Gareth? I don't know your brothers very well, and I'm not very clever. Well, which?

GAWAIN. Gaheris.

QUEEN. And as welcome here as you are yourself.

> [*She kisses the startled* GAHERIS. *Then she fills a cup for herself.*]

My magnificent nephews! The roof and walls of my

house for your comfort, and my heart for you.

> [*She drinks the toast to them. They are charmed by her kindness.*]

GAWAIN. Slainte mhath [*slawntu var*], my queen.

GAHERIS. Slainte!

> [*They drink to her in return.*]

And, madam—you'll keep our secret?

GAWAIN. Of course she will.

QUEEN. You mean—the secret about——?

GAHERIS. Me. It would be shaming if people knew that Gawain must use his own brother for a servant.

QUEEN. Torture would not wring it from me.

> [KAY *comes into the room. He is planning to be very nice to Orkney. Perhaps the* KING *has given him a little talk.*]

KAY. Sir Gawain, I've arranged for you to have a pleasant room, and the fire is lighted there. If you'll come now, I'll show you——

> [*He sees the scatter of coins on the table.*]

Who's left this useless litter lying about?

> [GAWAIN *crosses to him.*]

GAWAIN. I was lightening my wallet of its trash. Take it, sir, for your trouble.

> [*He strides out of the room.* GAHERIS *gulps his wine down, and follows. When they are gone,* KAY *recovers his voice.*]

KAY. The devil take you and your insults, Orkney!

> [*The* QUEEN *intercepts him as he is about to follow the others off.*]

QUEEN. Kay! Kay—it was all they had. Why did you have to notice it?

KAY [*Pulling up sharply*]. Oh! I'm sorry. I wouldn't for all the world——

[32]

QUEEN. I know you wouldn't. And forget what he said. His pride was badly hurt. Go after him, before he loses himself in the castle. And—be kind, Kay. He's terrified of us all. Make it easier for him.

KAY. If he lets me.

> [*He smiles wryly at her, and goes out. The* QUEEN *wanders to the table, and inspects the coins.*]

QUEEN [*Gently*]. Roughly about four-and-six——

> [*The* KING *enters, with a pile of clothes in his arms.*]

KING. Oh. And where are my two nephews?

QUEEN [*Laughing*]. You knew the squire, then?

KING. Gaheris? He came with Gawain last time—as his page.

QUEEN. Well, he's about to rook the castle servants at some terrible Orkney version of "Find the Lady".

KING. He hasn't changed much, either. He did that before. The poor dears were always broke, and would never admit it.

> [*He prods the heap of coins idly, and grins at the* QUEEN.]

I've financed a couple of lads to lose a decent amount to him.

QUEEN. I wonder why we always under-estimate you, Arthur?

> [*The* KING *goes to the door, carrying the clothes. The* QUEEN *picks up the tray of food, and joins him there. They look, for a moment, like two patient servants.*]

KING. If we're very, very careful, do you think Gawain will settle down quietly, now?

[33]

QUEEN. Well—they say hope is cheap.
    [*They turn to go off.*]

CURTAIN

THE SAME, TWO DAYS LATER

The KING *is standing by the window, down left, which is now wide open. The snow has stopped, and the light outside is brilliant. He looks both amused and concerned by what he is watching. A certain amount of noise is going on below. The* QUEEN *enters.*

QUEEN. Heavens, it's cold in here! You've got the window wide open. Bruno, are you mad? You'll catch your death!

> [*She crosses, while speaking, and now she sees what is happening outside.*]

What *are* they doing? Fighting? Who is it?

KING. Kay and Gawain. They're only playing.

QUEEN. Oh, how silly! Look at the horses sliding in the snow. Someone will get hurt.

KING. They're using padded spears. No sword-play. I've forbidden that. If anyone falls, the snow will cushion them. And no armour, you see? Padded jackets, and leather helmets——

QUEEN. I don't want Kay knocked about.

KING. He's more likely to come off best. A sword is Gawain's weapon. He isn't so good on horseback. It's not his way of fighting. And old Kay is crafty with a spear—oh, he's done it! There goes Gawain!

QUEEN. [*Averting her eyes*]. Is he all right?

KING. Yes, he's rolling over. Gaheris is picking him up. Kay's dismounted and gone to help——

> [*He stops, and murmurs "Now, now!". Then he leans out of the window.*]

Gawain! None of that! I said no swords. Yes, I'm watching you. So I should think!

> [*He turns back into the room, to hide a smile.*]

Cheeky devil! I'll give him "slipped his memory"!

QUEEN. May we have the window shut?

KING. What, dear? Oh, yes, it's all over. They're coming in, now.

> [*He closes the window. The* QUEEN *has gone over to the fireplace.*]

QUEEN. You've got him, haven't you? Like whistling a tame hawk to your wrist.

KING. Wild one. Yes, I've got him—if I watch him twenty-five hours a day.

QUEEN [*Feeling rather left out*]. Sometimes I wish I were a man.

KING. Oh, come! I might understand you better, but not like you more.

QUEEN. Ah—liking——

KING [*Briskly*]. Now look, dear, when Gawain tells us that his horse slipped——

QUEEN. Which it did, sometime *before* he fell off.

KING. Exactly. It won't be quite a lie.

> [*They both laugh.* GAHARIS *enters, and bows in the doorway.*]

Everything under control, Torcull?

GAHERIS. Yes, sir. My lord Gawain sent me to say he'll come as soon as he's changed his clothes—and stopped his nose bleeding.

KING. Shouldn't you be putting a key down his back, or something?

GAHERIS. He won't let me. He's vexed with me for telling Sir Kay I fixed a stirrup badly, so that it slipped.

KING. Did you?

GAHERIS. Well, something slipped.

QUEEN. You spoil him, Torcull.

GAHERIS. Someone must.

QUEEN. He needs a wife.

> [GAHERIS *is about to leave the room, but this remark brings him round.*]

GAHERIS. He'll marry no mortal woman.

QUEEN. He'll have his work cut out to marry anything else!

KING. Gah—Torcull, come here!

> [GAHERIS *is again half-way through the door. He turns enquiringly.*]

Don't make that sort of remark, and stroll away. What on earth did you mean?

GAHERIS. That the Prince Gawain should wed a swan-

[37]

woman, sir, or a seal-woman, or one from the Sidhe [*Shee*]. May I go, now?

KING. No. How dare you leave such a statement hanging in the air?

GAHERIS [*Calmly*]. I only meant that if he wedded a fairy-woman, she would find her swan's-feathers again, or her seal-skin, and be away back to the waters, or into the Hollow Hills, before she broke her heart. The High Queen has frozen his for other women.

QUEEN [*Rather nettled*]. We'll see about that.

GAHERIS. You'd need to break the Hills, madam.

KING. Yes—yes. Run along, Torcull.

    [*He is suddenly deep in thought.* GAHERIS *bows and departs.*]

QUEEN. A seal-woman! Living in the bath, and smelling of fish!

KING. I know what he meant, though. We really need Merlyn's advice. Pity he decided to retire.

QUEEN. A very good thing, the terrible old man! He was a bad influence. He muddled people. I was glad he went away, with his dreams of old pagan magic.

KING. You think magic is only a dream?

QUEEN. Don't you?

    [*Being out of her depth in such moonshine, she is a bit irritable.*]

Surely there's enough to worry about in real life, without starting on fantasies! For civilised people, the Hollow Hills are sealed.

    [*The room begins to grow darker. The* KING *glances uneasily round him.*]

What's the matter, Bruno?

KING. Be careful, Guinevere. There could be listeners.

QUEEN. What sort of——?

KING. Talking of things sometimes attracts their attention. If you open your mind to darkness, it's like opening a window to the night.

QUEEN. I don't want any windows opened at the moment!

> [*She goes over to the window, down right. The room is darker still. A high, thin, whistling noise comes from somewhere near the fireplace. Neither she nor the* KING *hears this.*]

It's going to snow again, I suppose. Strange how the weather in Britain always takes one by surprise.

> [*She is trying to get the conversation back to ordinary levels. The whistle starts again. This time the* KING *hears it, though not distinctly.*]

You'd think, after all the years we've endured it——

KING. Listen.

> [*A pause. The whistling dies away.*]

QUEEN. Listen to what, Bruno?

KING. I thought—It must have been a bird flying over the roof.

> [*Light comes slowly back into the room.*]

QUEEN. There, and it didn't snow, after all. The cloud's blown away. It was only a threat.

KING. From outside?

> [KAY *enters, fastening his collar, having changed his clothes from those he wore to joust. He speaks cheerfully.*]

KAY. I'll be as stiff as a board for a week! Why did I let myself get talked into that frolic?

QUEEN. You were splendid.

KAY. Not bad, for a retired old fogy! I couldn't take him with a sword, though.

KING. I hope you don't intend to try.

KAY. Did you see——? Yes, of course. You reined him in.

KING. Had he lost his temper?

KAY. Mislaid it for a moment. His face changed, before you shouted at him. But, for that moment, it was like seeing a window open into darkness.

KING. The shadow of his home—at the back of the North Wind——

KAY. Hey! That's another term for death.

KING. I know. Also another term for Spiral Castle—Cobweb Castle—the House of the Witch, in the Perilous Lands——

QUEEN. Please, Bruno! Whatever's got into you?

KING. All that talk about the Old Hills. It sent out my thoughts to shadowy places.

QUEEN. Meaning no disrespect, dear, there's a side of your family that's better left in the shade!

KING. Do you still wish I'd left Gawain there?

KAY. Actually, I'm getting quite fond of him, in a guarded way. He makes me feel younger. Do you know what I said just now, when I picked him up? I said "Yah to you, laddie!"

QUEEN. Bruno, I'm *devoted* to him! As long as he leaves his Celtic twilight well behind him, not trailing it like a cloak at his heels!

> [GAWAIN *comes into the room. He now wears a tunic, not unlike that of the* KING. *It does, in fact, belong to the* KING.]

Oh, my dear, are you all right?

GAWAIN. I'm fine, auntie. Just bumped my nose.

[*He sounds quite happy about it. And now he crosses down to* KAY.]

Will you teach me that artful little trick, sir? It caught me clean off balance.

KING. Where's your squire?

GAWAIN. Just outside, sir.

KING. Bring him in.

[GAWAIN *goes to the door, and shouts to the passage outside.*]

GAWAIN. Gaheris! Thig thusa! [*Heeg hoosa*].

[*He realises instantly the name he has used, and swings round to face the* KING, *as* GAHERIS *enters and comes to him.*]

GAHERIS. My lord?

[*There is a slight pause.*]

KING. May we assume this is no unknown squire called Torcull, but your brother Sir Gaheris?

GAHERIS [*Quickly*]. It was my idea. Don't blame him.

GAWAIN. I told no lie. He *is* my squire, for the moment, and his second name is Torcull.

KING. Gawain——

[*He is trying not to laugh, and manages at last to say gravely:*]

Gawain, would you define your idea of a downright, black lie?

GAWAIN. Well—if I'd said "this is *not* my brother, and his name is *not* Gaheris——"

KING. Which would have hinted at the truth.

GAWAIN. Which is why one can't be too careful about lying.

[41]

QUEEN. Now that we all know where we are, why don't we play a nice simple game—like "Hide and Seek"!

KAY. Or "Hop-Scotch"?

[*The room begins to darken again.*]

There's a cold draught from somewhere.

[*The high, thin whistling begins again.* GAWAIN *and* GAHERIS *hear it, but none of the others. The Orkneys look hunted, and* GAWAIN *clutches his brother's arm. The others notice this. The room grows darker still, though bright sunlight still shows at the window. The* KING *speaks quietly.*]

KING. What can you hear, Gawain?

[*The* QUEEN *gives a startled exclamation.*]

GAWAIN [*Softly*]. Oh, no!

KAY. What's getting at you two?

[*The* KING *gestures him to silence. The whistling, which had died away, now recommences.* GAWAIN *goes towards it, and* GAHERIS *intercepts him.*]

GAHERIS. Don't answer it!

GAWAIN. I have to.

[*He goes to the tapestry downstage of the fireplace, and lifts a tassel from among its folds. He glances at the* KING *in acute embarrassment.*]

Will you excuse me, sir? [*To the tassel*] This is Gawain.

[*Now a high, faint, twittering noise comes from it, with no distinguishable words, and he holds a conversation with it.*]

Yes, of course I've got here. How could I answer, otherwise? Well—och, I'm sorry if I was impolite, mother. Yes, he's with me. May he stay? Please, mother——

[GAHERIS, *looking furious, marches down to him, and speaks hotly.*]

GAHERIS. Tell her I'm staying, whatever she may——!

[GAWAIN *restrains him with his free hand, and continues his conversation.*]

GAWAIN. He's sending you his love, mother, and——

QUEEN [*Indignantly, under her breath*]. I don't believe it! How dare she?

KING [*Equally indignant, though slightly amused*]. Ssh, dear.

GAWAIN. No—they've been kind. Why should they be pretending? I've not been here long enough to make them dislike me much. Maybe. What? Yes, she's—she's—pretty. Well, *you* are, of course! Dyed? No, I don't think so. Yes, I'll write. Yes, I'll be careful. Yes. Goodbye, mother.

[*He lets the tassel fall back on its cord. The room regains its proper light. A pause.*]

I'm—sorry about that. She does it whenever I'm from her sight!

GAHERIS. What did she say about me?

GAWAIN. You may stay.

GAHERIS. I would, anyway! The old——!

[*He breaks off and moves away left, very angrily.*]

KING. You should have made her happy by saying we were all horrible.

GAWAIN. You may laugh, my lord!

[*The* KING *goes to him, and speaks soothingly.*]

KING. Now, now. It's natural enough for her to concern herself with your well-being. And kind of her to—to get in touch.

QUEEN. Kind!

GAHERIS. As if we were bairns!

KING. She probably doesn't mean to be so possessive——
> [*The room darkens again, more quickly and eerily than before.*]

QUEEN. Not again!

KAY. She forgot to ask if he'd brushed his teeth properly.
> [*Everyone glances round uneasily.*]

KING [*To* GAWAIN]. Is that thing speaking? We couldn't hear it, you know.

GAWAIN. It is not.

KING. Then this time it probably is just a cloud coming over. The High Queen isn't the only source of shadow in the world.
> [*From somewhere far away comes the silvery sound of a horn blowing.*]

That's a hunting-horn.

GAHERIS. Blowing from where?

GAWAIN. Hunting what!

QUEEN. You two are deliberately trying to introduce an atmosphere of——
> [*Slowly, and of its own accord, the door swings open. The* GREEN KNIGHT *stands motionless outside. For a moment or two, there is utter silence. The others are rooted to the ground in stunned surprise.*
>
> *The* GREEN KNIGHT *is taller by a head than any man there. Everything about him is green, in varying shades, except for a holly-sprig on each of his upper arms, and his glowing red eyes. His hair and beard are green, so is his skin, and his clothes, and the antlered helmet with its metal nose-guard and cheek-pieces. He glitters with emeralds, set in greenish gold. His hands are*

[44]

*folded on the head of a great axe. The effect
is one of terrifying beauty. It is perfectly
obvious that the Hollow Hills have opened.*

The KNIGHT'S *speech and movements are never
hostile, though not naturalistic. He goes through
his ritual with dignity, icy aloofness, imper-
sonality, and courtesy. Occasionally, there is a
faintly ironic edge to his voice, as though, somewhere beneath the terrible exterior, lurks a dis-
tant amusement.*

*The Orkneys recover first. They are, perhaps,
more geared to this sort of thing.* GAWAIN *moves
in front of the* KING *and* QUEEN, *and* GAHERIS *is
at his side immediately. The* QUEEN, *a brave
woman, shows her shock only by her clenched
hands.* KAY *is at a loss. The* KING *puts on his
invisible mantle of royalty.*]

KNIGHT. Greeting, great king.

KING. Sir, you are welcome, if you come in peace.

GAWAIN. If not, I beg you give me time to arm.

KNIGHT. I am not here for battle. Were I so, who could
withstand me?

GAWAIN. I'll be happy to try.

KING. Gawain, go and attend the Queen. At once, please.

[*Unwillingly,* GAWAIN *crosses to the* QUEEN'S *side.*
GAHERIS *goes to the left of the door, alert and
watchful. The* KING *speaks calmly to the* KNIGHT.]

If you're not in arms, may we hope you mean to be
our guest? By what name may we greet you?

KNIGHT. By none—as yet. No guest should bring doom
to any house.

[GAWAIN *takes a step forward, but the* QUEEN
restrains him.]

[45]

KING. I see. And what doom have you brought here?

KNIGHT. The loss of your sword.

[*He stretches one hand towards the sword on the wall, and it slowly vanishes.*]

KAY. Sir, put that back!

KNIGHT. Impossible—at the moment.

KING. I'm not very sure of the protocol in these matters, but could you tell me in what way I've offended you? You are, of course, not human.

KNIGHT. My motive must stay secret. And I am, of course, not human.

KING. I've never been hostile to—your kind. Couldn't you satisfy your motive by some other means? That isn't just *any* sword, you know. It's a sort of symbol to my people. Of leadership and victory. They set some store by it. This land is hard-pressed, and needs whatever assurance it can find.

KNIGHT. The deed is done.

KING. Oh, surely not irrevocably? There's usually some way round these—incidents. A favour—a riddle—a deed——?

KNIGHT. A riddle.

KING. Well, I'm not good at them.

KNIGHT. You are allowed to consult others, to find the answer.

KING. Thank you. That gives me a better chance. Shall we get it over now? Then perhaps you'll stay to supper—?

KNIGHT. What does a woman most desire in all the world?

KING. How should I know? Oh, is that it?

KNIGHT. That is it.

[*A slight pause.*]

KING. Well, she—she—er—she——

[46]

[*He comes to a baffled halt, and then looks appealingly at the* QUEEN.]

Vera, what *does* a woman want most?

QUEEN [*Shortly*]. Peace and quiet!

KNIGHT. Not exclusively.

KING. Kay, what's your guess?

KAY. Merely from observation, fine clothes and jewels.

KNIGHT. Not deliberately.

KING. Gawain?

GAWAIN. Their own beauty.

KNIGHT. Not consistently.

GAHERIS. Obedient puppets for children!

KNIGHT. Not necessarily.

KING. Perhaps—love?

KNIGHT. Not primarily.

QUEEN [*In a rush*]. To be the first in a man's heart! To be the only and eternal reality for one man.

[*A slight pause.*]

KNIGHT. Not universally.

KING [*After a moment*]. May I question more people? Or must you have your answer here and now?

KNIGHT. On one condition, you may have a year to find the answer. And keep your sword meantime.

KING. What condition?

KNIGHT. A husband for my sister from among your knights.

KING. I can't lay a command of marriage on any of my men.

KNIGHT. Not *any* of your men, sir. One specifically. Your heir.

KING. No!

KNIGHT. You'll lose your only chance?

KING. Under that condition—yes, let the sword go.

GAWAIN [*Quietly from where he stands*]. I will marry your sister, sir.

KING. You will not!

GAWAIN. I pledge my word, knight. It's not been broken—often. It won't be this time.

QUEEN. But—you don't know what she may be like!

GAWAIN. Does that matter?

QUEEN [*To* KNIGHT]. Where is this lady?

KNIGHT. She will come.

> [*He holds out one hand towards the* KING. *He is holding the sword in it.*]

That promise gives you a year to answer my riddle. Fail, and the sword will vanish for ever.

KING [*Dully*]. Kay——

> [KAY *goes to the* KNIGHT *and takes the sword from him.*]

KAY. Will you leave us now, sir?

> [*A pause.*]

KNIGHT. It saddens me to cast a shade over your Yuletide merrymaking.

KAY. Your feelings do you credit. But I doubt if your continued presence will do much to relieve the gloom.

KNIGHT. Oh, I don't know.

KAY. You have in mind some further entertainment?

KNIGHT. Merely a Christmas game. The world knows the reputation of your fighting-men, King Arthur. The most valiant ever bred. To prove it no minstrel's tale, will any in your household be so hardy in spirit—so reckless and so bold—as to take up a challenge from me——

QUEEN. Please, no!

KNIGHT. Be at ease, madam. I said—a game.

KAY. Come to it, sir.

KNIGHT. I offer this axe to any man, to strike one blow at me. A blow I will suffer, unresisting, if he will then accept—unarmed and consenting—one blow in return, from the same axe.

[*A pause. The* KNIGHT *gives a scornful laugh.*]

What? Will no man play my game?

KING. If you truly seek folly, you will find it. Give me your axe. I'll be fool enough to strike you your blow.

KNIGHT. And stand for the return?

KING. Naturally.

GAHERIS. ⎱ Sir, let me—!
KAY. ⎰ I'll take it on!

[*As the* KING *takes the axe,* GAWAIN *speaks quietly to the* QUEEN.]

GAWAIN. Will you allow me to leave your side, madam?

[*Taking her consent for granted, he goes to the* KING.]

KING. Go away, Gawain!

GAWAIN. My lord, this affair is too foolish for you to tackle. I know how low my reputation stands. Nothing can cheapen it further. It cannot dishonour me to take up this childish challenge. Unless—unless, sir, you think me too far beneath contempt to be trusted with so small a task. If this is so, refuse my humble request.

KING. You've managed to make that impossible, haven't you? I didn't credit you with such low cunning.

GAWAIN [*Meekly*]. Thank you, sir. May I have the axe?

[*The* KING, *looking disapproving, is about to give it to him, but hesitates.*]

[49]

KING. Gawain, be careful, will you? This is a test of some sort.

GAWAIN. Instruct me, if you've no faith in my wit.

KING. I'll have a little talk with you later.

> [*He gives him the axe, and turns away to the fireplace.*]

GAWAIN [*To the* KNIGHT]. Will this substitute content you, sir?

KNIGHT. Sir, it charms me. I'll take off my helmet, and stand unguarded to your blow.

GAWAIN. You are too tall.

KNIGHT. I can kneel. It is your right to set the odds. And mine to hold you to them in your turn.

GAWAIN. And since the Queen is in no mood for violence —even in jest—let us go outside.

KNIGHT. As you please.

GAWAIN [*To the others*]. Will you excuse us?

> [*Getting no reply, he bows, and follows the* GREEN KNIGHT *out.* GAHERIS *goes, too, closing the door behind them. A pause. Light filters back into the room.*]

KING. I should have stopped him. But how could I? He tied me into knots with that performance of mock humility. I could hardly agree with it.

KAY. It would have served him right.

KING. If I had, and the tale got round, he'd never have lived it down.

QUEEN. Which of us would spread the tale?

KING. Who could answer for the Green Knight?

KAY. Gawain seems happy enough about it—so far.

> [*He is looking out of the window, down left, with great interest.*]

KING. But this is no ordinary challenge. It might have a terrible back-lash if not properly handled.

QUEEN. It can't possibly be happening! It's like Merlyn at his worst.

KAY. Come and see this!

> [*The* QUEEN *turns away. The* KING *remains sunk in uneasy thoughts. There is a noise outside the window, as though a small crowd has gathered.*]

KING. If a man—or one who wears the appearance of a man—offers to endure a blow unarmed, then in ordinary courtesy only the lightest tap should be inflicted.

> [*There is a shout outside the window.* KAY *turns back into the room.*]

He's done it?

KAY [*Dryly*]. He has, indeed.

KING. If he hurt the Knight, in any way, he must endure the same.

KAY. He's safe enough.

KING. Well, you relieve me. I was very much afraid he might not realise——

> [GAHERIS *enters and holds the door open.* GAWAIN *comes in quickly, looking pleased with himself. He has the axe in one hand, and the head of the* GREEN KNIGHT *in the other.*]

No!

GAWAIN. One stroke, sir!

> [*The* QUEEN *gives an exclamation, and covers her eyes.*]

Oh, I'm sorry, Auntie Vera. I shouldn't have brought it in.

[51]

KAY. You shouldn't have been let out!

KING. Gawain, you were meant to touch him lightly. Then he could only have done the same to you.

GAWAIN. He can't do that much, now. He can do no harm at all, now. Nor will he return in a year's time, so your sword is safe, whether you find the riddle's answer or no.

KING. I'd rather have risked the sword than risk you!

GAWAIN. Och, I'm in no danger.

> [*The room darkens. The door opens. The* GREEN KNIGHT *stands headless in the doorway. A pause. The* KNIGHT *beckons slowly to* GAWAIN. *Another pause. Then he beckons again, and* GAWAIN *goes and gives him the severed head. He settles it comfortably on his left arm, and speaks calmly:*]

KNIGHT. Thank you. The riddle stands. The challenge stands. I summon you, Sir Gawain, to the return stroke.

> [*A slight pause.*]

Or will you break your word?

GAWAIN. Outside then.

KING. Now wait!

> [*He speaks appealingly to the* KNIGHT.]

You're within your rights, but—give him a little time.

KNIGHT. I am not merciless. As I gave a year's grace to you, so will I to your knight. [*To* GAWAIN] In a year's time, sir, I lay it upon you to meet me, and take such a blow as you have dealt to me.

QUEEN [*To Knight*]. There is the matter of your sister——

KNIGHT. She will wed the heir of Britain, on the word of Prince Gawain.

QUEEN [*Persisting*]. But if you behead him——

KNIGHT. Who is the next heir?

[52]

GAHERIS [*Blankly*]. Well, I am.

KNIGHT. Will you uphold your brother's word?

GAHERIS. Always!

KNIGHT. Then the future of my sister is not in question, whatever the future of Sir Gawain. He need not fear that I will favour him.

GAWAIN. I fear neither your favour nor your axe.

KNIGHT. The time is not yet on you. You may feel otherwise at midnight on the eve of next New Year, when you come alone to the Green Chapel, to keep our tryst there.

GAWAIN. Where will I find it?

KNIGHT. Search. And search alone.

GAWAIN. And if I fail to find it?

KNIGHT. Then you'll be foresworn.

GAWAIN. Your name might be a help to me.

KNIGHT. I am known as the Knight of the Green Chapel.

GAWAIN. You set me an impossible task!

KNIGHT. Did you, who are acquainted with the dark, think it would be easy?

> [*He turns the head on his arm, so that it seems to look at the other humans.*]

Remember, king, a year goes quickly by.

> [*He holds out his free hand for the axe, which* GAWAIN *gives him.*]

Remember, sir, a year goes quickly by.

> [*The* KNIGHT *stalks quietly from the room. The door closes. Light returns, but it is now that of early evening.*]

GAWAIN. Gaheris, come and arm me. Quickly!

GAHERIS. Now?

GAWAIN. What chance have I to find his lair, unless I follow now?

> [*As he moves towards the door, a horn blows faintly. The door opens, and a veiled lady is standing there. Her dress is green, patterned with holly-sprays. There are emeralds glittering in the folds of her skirt, and on her sleeves. She is small and slender and graceful, with beautiful hands, and a cool young voice. This is the* LADY RAGNELL.]

Let me pass, lady, for I'm in great haste.

RAGNELL. No need, sir. My brother has gone by a road you cannot follow.

GAWAIN. Your——? Then you——? Has he told you— I have promised——?

> [*He is, for once, at a loss for words. She comes further into the room.*]

RAGNELL. To wed me. I know, Gawain of Orkney. And failing you——

GAHERIS [*Dismally*]. Me.

GAWAIN. Both of us—I mean, either of us, will be honoured——

QUEEN [*Firmly taking charge*]. You are welcome, fair lady. May we know your name?

RAGNELL. I am Ragnell, madam.

> [*Slowly she puts back her veil. Her long hair is white, streaked with green. One sad eye slants hideously upwards, the other downwards. Her nose is long and crooked. Her mouth is a twisted, crimson gash in a fish-pale, greenish face. She is awful to see, and pathetic. Her thoughts, at this moment, can only be guessed,*

[54]

after the fashion of the Sidhe. She speaks calmly.]

I am also called The Loathly Lady.

[*After a moment,* GAWAIN *pulls himself together. He says with some care:*]

GAWAIN. Well—I fear I must go, now. With only a year to find the Chapel——

GAHERIS. Forbye the Lady can direct you there? Then you can stay, and—and——

GAWAIN [*Severely*]. That would be cheating. I've been told to search. We will neither of us cheat, Gaheris.

GAHERIS. Yes, but—yes, very well. I've made my promise.

GAWAIN [*To* RAGNELL]. Will you go to my mother's house, to wait?

RAGNELL. To my own place, sir. I know your lady-mother.

[GAWAIN *crosses to the* KING.]

GAWAIN. Have I your leave to go?

[*The* KING *looks at him, nods briefly, touches his arm, and turns away.*]

QUEEN [*To* GAWAIN]. For the love of heaven, try to be careful, my dear!

GAWAIN. If it rests with me.

[*Moving towards the door, he encounters* KAY.]

KAY. I can only keep my fingers crossed for you.

GAWAIN. It will help greatly, sir, I'm sure.

[*He goes to the door, followed by his brother, then he hesitates, and comes back to* RAGNELL.]

Under the circumstances, it's scarcely in order to ask for your good wishes——

RAGNELL. They are yours, sir, without asking. May you meet all the luck that you deserve.

[*For some reason known only to himself,* GAWAIN *finds this funny.*]

[55]

GAWAIN. Thank you very much.

> [*He goes out, grinning, with* GAHERIS. *A slight pause.*]

RAGNELL [*Lightly*]. I hope he does come back. I like him.

> [*Another pause.*]

KING. Well, don't all look at *me!* What could I do?

CURTAIN

A ROOM IN A NORTHUMBERLAND CASTLE

All that can be seen at first is a mass of thin, fine hangings that are swinging and swaying, green and blue and gold, under flickering lights. Perhaps they are tapestries, swirling in a high wind. Perhaps it is all seen in the mind of a half-conscious man. Perhaps it is caused by ancient magic. There comes a sound of horns blowing, far-off and sweet. Through them a voice speaks like an echo. A man's voice, but somehow not human.

VOICE. Gawain ... Gawain ... Gawain ...

It is now possible to see, up left centre, a couch covered with fur rugs, where GAWAIN *is lying. A dark figure leans over him. He moves his head, and tries to lift himself on one elbow. Instantly, all movement and sound in the*

[57]

room cease. The light becomes a normal one for early
evening. The room is only a room, hung with tapestries.
A door, down right, might almost be the Narberth window,
with slight alterations. The window, down left, is exactly
like the Narberth one. Up right is a small table, set with
flagon and cups, and a chair beside it. The dark figure that
seemed to be looming rather gloatingly over GAWAIN, *now*
turns out to be a lady. She presses him gently back on the
cushion, and seats herself on a stool near by.
The LADY MIRIEL *is sparklingly beautiful, with nothing*
conventional about her beauty. Her black hair is bound
up with dull gold ribbons, and a similar ribbon is round
the waist of her grey-and-white dress. She can change
mood as swiftly as a spring morning. Some of the time,
she is playing a game that amuses her, and some of the
time she is quite sincere. It is not easy to tell when she
will change manner. At the moment, she is being The
Perfect Hostess. She speaks reassuringly:

MIRIEL. Sir Gawain——

> [*He looks at her blankly, and she takes his hand.*
> GAWAIN *is now wearing a yellow tunic, and a fur*
> *rug is draped over him.*]

Be at ease, sir. You're safe in my house.

GAWAIN [*Muttering*]. My head's ringing.

MIRIEL. It will, if you thresh about so. Lie still.

GAWAIN. I can't move my arm!

MIRIEL. It's badly bruised. You had a fall.

GAWAIN. There was a—white castle—among trees——

MIRIEL. You're in that castle, now.

GAWAIN. Dogs—fine great hounds—across my path. A
hunting-horn. My horse—he got in a panic. He's not a
panicky sort of horse——

[58]

MIRIEL. Keep still.

GAWAIN. I fell off!

MIRIEL. Yes, and struck your head and arm on a tree-root. No blame to you, sir. My husband is a wild hunter, and any fault is his. He brought you in, and now you are our guest, and most welcome.

GAWAIN. But I must go on. I have a tryst to keep.

MIRIEL. There's time enough.

> [*He tries to sit up, and clutches his head, with a groan.*]

GAWAIN. The top's coming off!

MIRIEL. No, it's just dented.

> [*Down left, the door opens to admit* SIR BERCILAK. *He is a splendid-looking man, with a friendly, rugged personality that can be somewhat over-powering at times. He is dressed in black and white, and his black hair is thrown back carelessly from a weather-tanned face. He moves restlessly, giving the impression that this room—perhaps the whole castle—is too small for him. He laughs easily and loudly. He resembles a great hunting-hound, extravert and kindly, but occasionally still and concentrated as though he waits for a quarry to break from cover.*
>
> SIR BERCILAK *and his wife never actually say or do anything that might not be put down to human feelings, yet from time to time there is a hint of some more sinister under-current.*]

BERCILAK [*Heartily*]. How fares our guest?

> [*His ringing voice goes through* GAWAIN'S *aching head like an arrow.*]

[59]

GAWAIN. Not good.

MIRIEL. He won't improve for being bellowed at.

BERCILAK. I'm muzzled.

> [*She goes to the table to pour wine for him, and he stares at* GAWAIN.]

Blame me for your mishap, sir. Careering about and startling your good horse from his wits.

GAWAIN. Is he——?

BERCILAK. Quite recovered. And guzzling his head off in the stable. He fared better than you. I thought I'd killed you, till I got you here.

GAWAIN. How long have I——?

MIRIEL. You were unconscious for two hours, and then you slept. It's evening now, and night coming on.

GAWAIN. I must go.

> [*He tries to sit up again, but* BERCILAK *prevents him.* MIRIEL *gives a cup to her husband, and brings another to* GAWAIN.]

MIRIEL. Try to drink some of this. It's only milk.

> [*She holds it to his mouth, and he drinks some.*]

GAWAIN. It tastes odd.

MIRIEL. There's a herb steeped in it, to soothe pain and bring sleep.

GAWAIN. No—I must ride on.

BERCILAK [*Affably ignoring this*]. You are the Prince of Orkney, Sir Gawain.

GAWAIN. Yes. How did you——?

BERCILAK. I'm no court knight, but I can read the blazon on a shield, sir; and yours was fastened on your saddle. We're deeply honoured, and will not let you go till you're fully recovered. I am Sir Bercilak, of Hautdesert in the Mountains of Northumberland, and this is my wife, the Lady Miriel.

GAWAIN. You're both extremely kind. But I cannot accept your——

MIRIEL. You shouldn't try to talk.

> [*But* GAWAIN *has collected a little strength, and makes an effort to explain.*]

GAWAIN. The Eve of New Year is only three days off. By then I must find an unknown place, for which I've already searched the land.

BERCILAK. What place?

GAWAIN. Has any tale reached you of a Green Chapel— and the Green Knight who has his being there?

> [*A pause*].

BERCILAK [*Quietly*]. The Green Chapel.

MIRIEL [*Under her breath*]. The Green Knight.

> [*Another pause. They both look at* GAWAIN *and smile.*]

BERCILAK. Not two miles from here. Your travels are over, sir. You've three whole days to recover your strength, and then I'll show you the way.

GAWAIN. That's unbelievable luck!

BERCILAK [*Cheerfully*]. Luck strikes like lightning where least expected. And now you must do what we think best for you, eh?

GAWAIN. Under your roof, sir, I'm at your command.

MIRIEL. And at mine?

GAWAIN. At yours under any roof, my lady.

> [*He falls back wearily against the cushion.* BERCILAK *and* MIRIEL *look at one another across his head.*]

MIRIEL. Then my first command, is that you drink some more milk.

[61]

> [*She holds the cup for him to do so.*]

It will bring sleep through the coming night, and most
of tomorrow.

> [BERCILAK *has gone to the window, and stands
> there looking out.*]

BERCILAK. The snow has settled. The wind has died. I'll
be away to my hunting again, in the dawn. It's a pity
you're in no shape to join me, Sir Gawain, but my
lady will entertain you till I return.

> [*He stretches his arms, and says with great
> joviality:*]

This is a festive season, sir. Shall we make a wager, for
your amusement and mine?

MIRIEL. He's half asleep. He didn't hear you.

GAWAIN. I heard.

BERCILAK. Prince, you have laid yourself under my command, and it's my fancy to play a Yuletide game. A
wager, as I said. Whatever I take in my hunting, I'll
give to you to use as you please. In fair exchange, you
shall give me whatever may fall to your fortune.
Agreed?

GAWAIN. You'll fare poorly. What chance have I for
winnings?

BERCILAK. Fall as it may befall. Pledge me your faith, as
I mine to you.

> [*He raises his cup of wine, and* GAWAIN *his cup
> of milk, and they drink.* MIRIEL *pulls the fur rug
> gently over* GAWAIN. *He glances a bit uneasily
> from one to the other of his hosts, then shuts his
> eyes. The others smile. They move downstage,
> and take hands formally at arms' length.*]

MIRIEL. Night is here.

BERCILAK. Darken the room for sleep.

> [*They go together to the door. As they go out, the room darkens, and lights begin to flicker on tapestries that slowly wave. A horn sounds its distant music. Through this, the voice speaks again like an echo:*]

VOICE. Darkness and sleep—and sleep—and time goes over——

> [*After a while,* GAWAIN *stirs and groans and lifts his head. All other movement in the room ceases, and all sound. The light turns to evening light.* GAWAIN *sits up with an effort. Then, hearing a sound outside the door, he lies down again.* MIRIEL *enters quietly. There is something more youthful and demure about her appearance. She has a fine white veil round hair and chin, and her ribbon belt is blue. She carries a covered dish and a beaker, which she sets on the table. She is being a Simple, Innocent Young Lady.*]

MIRIEL. Good-morrow, Sir Gawain.

> [*He does not move, and she gives a soft laugh.*]

Well! I'm glad you feel so safe in my house that you let yourself be caught unaware.

> [GAWAIN *decides to wake up.*]

GAWAIN. Why should I feel unsafe, good lady?

MIRIEL. Oh, you heard me, in your sound sleep? I wouldn't advise you to be too sure of your safety. See!

> [*She holds the rug down over him, pinning his arms under it.*]

You're my prisoner. Who'd believe I could capture such a knight—single-handed!

[63]

GAWAIN. I can only surrender, and sue for mercy.

MIRIEL. No woman is constrained by rules of chivalry.

GAWAIN. Surely by those of mercy?

MIRIEL. Not always. But I'll consider accepting ransom, in due course. Meanwhile—you are free!

> [*She releases him, and goes to the table. Then she turns in girlish dismay.*]

Oh, I'm sorry! I forgot to ask how you're feeling today.

GAWAIN. Better, thank you.

MIRIEL. I've brought you some food.

> [*He starts to get to his feet.*]

No, no, you mustn't! Let me wait on you.

GAWAIN. And risk such another ambush?

> [*She giggles. He manages to get to the table, and sits in the chair. She takes the cover off the bowl.*]

MIRIEL [*With simple pride*]. Porridge, I'm sure you like that.

GAWAIN. It could depend what herbs are steeped in it.

MIRIEL. It's nothing but oats and water and salt. Am I a witch?

GAWAIN. Ladies are so versatile. My own mother——

MIRIEL. I am not your mother!

GAWAIN. Then I'll trust my gentle hostess.

> [*He starts eating the porridge. She suddenly gives a huge sigh, which surprises him. She clasps her hands dramatically together.*]

MIRIEL [*Gleefully*]. How every lady in the world would envy me, being here like this with you.

GAWAIN. Why?

MIRIEL. Their jealousy would scratch out my eyes. Me! Talking to you! No one near to interrupt or eavesdrop. Poor, silly, ignorant Miriel, and the noble Prince Gawain—honoured by all the world for knightly valour and high courtesy——

GAWAIN [*Coldly*]. You mock a man who has already asked for mercy. Beauty should also be kind.

MIRIEL [*Rapturously*]. Oh, do you truly think me beautiful?

GAWAIN. Don't you?

[*She is momentarily checked, but rallies fast.*]

MIRIEL. I fear you think me very simple.

GAWAIN. Far from it, madam.

MIRIEL. A poor, simple, young girl, living far from the world, finds herself helpless in the hands of a clever man.

GAWAIN. It's a shame.

MIRIEL [*Rallying again*]. I've long dreamed of a—friend like you.

GAWAIN. Och, too great an honour, to be friend to you and Sir Bercilak.

MIRIEL. I would that you had been my lord.

GAWAIN. I fear you mock my stupidity again.

MIRIEL. Sir, I am *more* stupid!

GAWAIN. Madam, I am practically half-witted.

[*They give each other unbelievably stupid stares. Neither is impressed.*]

MIRIEL [*Shortly*]. If you were as dull as you pretend, you'd be locked up!

GAWAIN. It's often been suggested.

MIRIEL. You're laughing at me. You despise the hearts that are cast at your feet. But, all the same——

> [*She drops prettily at his feet, and gazes at him with kitten's eyes.*]

I am your servant, sir, to command as you will.

GAWAIN. Then please get up. It's I who am your servant, madam, and your husband's, too.

> [*He hauls her to her feet, a bit abruptly. She makes the best of it.*]

MIRIEL. Oh, how strong you are.

> [*He has an idea. He clutches his left arm, with a look of extreme agony.*]

GAWAIN. My arm! I forgot it was injured.

> [*This gets him nowhere. She runs to his aid, in tender distress.*]

MIRIEL. Lean on me. I'll help you to the couch.

GAWAIN [*Releasing himself*]. Your touch has cured the pain.

MIRIEL. Then, in return for that cure, say the words I long to hear.

GAWAIN. What words?

MIRIEL [*Bashfully*]. Must I prompt? The first word is "I". The third is "you". Surely you can supply the middle one?

> [*A pause*].

GAWAIN. Of course. I thank you. The kindness of Lady Miriel and the noble Bercilak has earned my deathless gratitude.

MIRIEL. I'm disappointed in you.

GAWAIN. And I'm sorry to hear it.

[66]

MIRIEL. You're not in the least sorry. You've deceived us cruelly. Why did you carry the shield of Gawain? You are not he.

GAWAIN. Then the thump on my head was worse than I thought.

MIRIEL. King Arthur's nephew would never forget when he owes ransom.

GAWAIN. Have you decided what it is?

MIRIEL. A kiss in courtesy.

GAWAIN. I cannot——

MIRIEL. You cannot, in courtesy, refuse.

GAWAIN [*Thinking hard*]. You're too generous, to pay my ransom for me. But I accept.

> [*As she approaches, he drops to one knee, and lowers his head so that she is obliged to kiss him on the brow.*]

You do remind me of my dear mother.

MIRIEL. How dare you!

GAWAIN [*Sentimentally insincere*]. When we were children, she would kiss me and my brothers so—when the mood took her.

> [*He gets up, and* MIRIEL *abandons some of her sweet girlishness.*]

MIRIEL. Shall I tell you something, Sir Gawain? If Bercilak's deer are as wary as you, we shall all go hungry!

GAWAIN. They only run for their lives.

> [*A hunting-horn blows outside the window. The door opens, and there is* BERCILAK *himself.* MIRIEL *runs to him.*]

MIRIEL. How went your chase?

BERCILAK. Splendidly.

[67]

[*He puts one arm round her, and looks amusedly at* GAWAIN.]

I'm glad to see you better, sir. And, since you're on your feet, come to the window, and see my trophies in the courtyard.

[*He goes and flings open the window.* GAWAIN *crosses to him.*]

There! Enough good venison for a month of fine feasting.

GAWAIN. You did well, sir.

BERCILAK. And, by the pledge we made, those spoils are yours. What will you do with them?

GAWAIN. May I give them to your kitchens, for your month's fine feasting?

[BERCILAK *laughs heartily, and thumps him between the shoulders. He buckles slightly under it.*]

MIRIEL. Sir Gawain needs careful handling.

BERCILAK. I'm a clumsy fool! Come and sit down.

[*He takes* GAWAIN *to the couch, and lets him down on it.*]

I see you have over-tried your strength.

[*He sits beside him, and says with anxious kindliness.*]

Yet I must remind you of our wager. Anything you've gained today is owed to me.

GAWAIN. By every right, Sir Bercilak.

[*Amused, he leans forward and kisses him lightly on the brow.*]

BERCILAK [*Laughing*]. You had sweet fortune, sir.

[*He rises, still laughing.* GAWAIN *leans back wearily on the cushion.*]

Where did you come by that?

GAWAIN. There was nothing in the contract about explanations. You have had all your due.

MIRIEL. And you are almost asleep.

GAWAIN [*Rousing*]. What was in that porridge, apart from oats and things?

MIRIEL. Nothing to harm you.

BERCILAK. You've still two days, to rest and recover strength. Too bad that you can't come hunting with me tomorrow. There's a great wild boar that's been harassing the countryside, and I mean to bring him to bay. My lady will see that you have another quiet day. And I'll try to bring you the monster's head. Perhaps you'll prosper, too.

GAWAIN [*Vaguely*] Touch wood, not.

> [BERCILAK *laughs, and pulls the rug over him.*
> *Then holds out his hand to* MIRIEL. *She takes it*
> *formally, and they move towards the door.*]

BERCILAK. Darkness falls again.

MIRIEL. The night is still.

> [*They go out. The room darkens. Lights flicker,*
> *and the tapestries swing and sway. The horn*
> *sounds its musical call, and the voice echoes it:*]

VOICE. Lie still—in darkness—time is passing by——

> [GAWAIN *stirs and groans. The room stills, and*
> *becomes silent. The light is that of evening.*
> GAWAIN *gets to his feet, and goes towards the*
> *window. The door flies open, and* MIRIEL *comes*
> *swiftly into the room. This time, she has a vivid*
> *and feline quality about her. Her eyes gleam*
> *wickedly. She wears a collar of bright red jewels,*
> *and a red-jewelled ribbon round her waist. Her*
> *hair is unbound. She is playing another role, that*

[69]

[*of Enchantress.* GAWAIN *observes all this, uneasily. He decides to take the offensive.*]

GAWAIN. Good-evening, my mild and gentle hostess.

MIRIEL. Fair sir, how do you feel today?

GAWAIN. Apprehensive. You should have sent servants to wake me before now.

MIRIEL. I did. They brushed your hair, and bathed you, and you never stirred.

[*He chokes slightly.* MIRIEL *goes to the table and touches a flagon, and a dish covered with a white cloth, newly set there. She speaks across her shoulder, with a smouldering smile.*]

I hope you'll be easier to entertain, after so sound a sleep!

[*She holds out one hand to him, enticingly, and he backs to the window.*]

Come nearer, Gawain.

GAWAIN. Fresh air is good for me.

MIRIEL. You're not, by any chance, afraid?

GAWAIN. No, no. This twitch is natural.

[*She glides over to him.*]

MIRIEL. What other tricks are natural to you?

[*He crosses quickly to the table. He looks at the covered dish.*]

GAWAIN. I'm not sure that I'm hungry.

MIRIEL. Don't flee before you're threatened.

[*She crosses to the table, and whips off the cover, and shows some boiled eggs.*]

There!

GAWAIN [*Weakly*]. Delicious.

MIRIEL. I aim to please.

[*He sits down quickly, and starts to eat the eggs, keeping a wary eye on the lady. Being, indeed,*

*stronger today, he finds her more amusing than
alarming. He is prepared to fence with her. She
circles round, smiling.*]

What shall we talk about?

GAWAIN. There's always the weather.

MIRIEL. And love.

GAWAIN. Of which I know nothing at all.

MIRIEL [*Lightly*]. Educating ignorance is one of the duties
of a gentlewoman.

> [*She sits on the table. He goes on with his supper
> firmly.*]

GAWAIN [*Equally lightly*]. And honour is one of the duties
of a knight. Is there some salt?

> [*She reaches behind her, grabs the salt container
> and set it before him with a bang. He starts, over-
> violently.*]

Thank you.

MIRIEL. Has no one told you, love has duties, too?

GAWAIN. People keep things from me.

> [*She leans along the table towards him. He gets
> up and goes to the window.*]

GAWAIN. It's cold in here, isn't it? I'll close the window.

> [*He does so. And turns back to her, politely.*]

I beg your pardon. I think I interrupted you.

MIRIEL. Where was I?

GAWAIN. Pouring across the table.

> [*He sits on the window-ledge, and grins at her.
> She narrows her eyes, and moves towards him
> in her most cat-like fashion.*]

MIRIEL. You will tell me if I'm boring you?

[71]

GAWAIN. You're very amusing.

MIRIEL. Amuse *me*.

GAWAIN. I cannot match your wit. And my throat's dry.
Is that wine on the table? I hate to trouble you——

> [*She is forced to turn and go back to the table
> to pour him some wine. She brings it to him,
> and stands very close as he takes a sip. He
> looks up at her.*]

Would you have me drink alone, lady?

> [*She goes quickly back and pours another cup
> of wine, and drinks it off.*]

MIRIEL. Does that calm your suspicious little mind?

GAWAIN. In the matter of herbs, yes.

> [*He then drinks his wine. She moves towards
> him while he does so.*]

MIRIEL. That may give you the courage to speak the words
I wish to hear.

> [*She leans on his shoulder, and he jumps up,
> dislodging her, and pretending to spill his wine.*]

GAWAIN. Now look what I've done! All over the fine
clothes that your dear husband lent me.

> [*She fetches the cloth that covered the eggs, and
> dabs tenderly at the breast of his tunic.*]

Allow me, madam.

> [*He takes the cloth from her, and becomes en-
> grossed in rubbing at some non-existent stain
> on his breast. She glares at him.*]

MIRIEL. I'll tell you something, Sir Gawain. If the wild
boar my husband hunts is as pig-headed as you——!

GAWAIN. I'm not a likeable character.

[*She holds out both hands to him. He puts the wine-cup into one, and the cloth into the other.*]
Thank you.

[*She throws the cloth at him, and he catches it. She turns away very quickly, and pretends to stumble, giving a small cry.* GAWAIN *automatically catches her to steady her, and she clutches him, remembering to hold the cup upright in her hand.*]

MIRIEL [*Piteously*]. I've twisted my ankle. Oh, what pain! I think I'm going to faint—help me to the couch——

[*He does so, and she sinks back on it with closed eyes. He takes the cup from her, and carefully pours the last drop of wine from it on to her face. She sits up with a yelp.*]

GAWAIN [*Anxiously*]. Shall I burn some feathers, madam?

MIRIEL. You're a monster!

[*She jumps up and goes towards the door. She is suddenly trying not to laugh. Then she turns to him.*]

What's more, you still owe me some ransom.

GAWAIN. You never said it was in instalments.

MIRIEL. Well, it is!

[*She comes back, laughing, and kisses him cheerfully on both cheeks.*]

GAWAIN. Just as my dear mother——

MIRIEL. You have a nerve of iron!

[*A hunting-horn is heard. The door opens, and* BERCILAK *enters.* MIRIEL *takes a few steps towards him.*]

I'm delighted to see you, my darling! How did you fare today?

[73]

BERCILAK. A hard chase after a stubborn quarry. Come, sir, and see the result.

[*He takes* GAWAIN *to the window.*]

There lies the monster. He led me a fine dance. I thought he'd have the best of it—but a good hunter doesn't give up easily. He finally turned at bay in some rushes by the lake, and I went in after him. It was an exciting skirmish! We were both down in the water, churning it all to mud——

[GAWAIN *dabs absently at his host's tunic with the cloth.*]

It's all right. Dried off on the ride home. Well, at last I got him—with one lunge, as fast as light! And there he lies below, with his great mouth snarling as he died. He'll turn any meal into a kingly feast, with an apple in that mouth.

GAWAIN. Delicious.

BERCILAK. He's yours, sir. What will you do with him?

GAWAIN. With your permission, give him to your kitchens, to add a kingly touch to some feast.

BERCILAK. Good. And now, Orkney, your due is paid.

GAWAIN. And I'll not grudge you yours.

[*He kisses* BERCILAK *cheerfully on both cheeks.*]

BERCILAK [*Laughing*]. You had sweet fortune, sir. I'll be hard put to it to match you, if you go on like this!

GAWAIN. Oh, I don't foresee——

[*A thin whistling noise comes from the hunting-horn slung round* BERCILAK'S *shoulder. They all hear it.* BERCILAK *pulls it round to the front of him, and it starts to twitter.*]

[74]

BERCILAK [*To* GAWAIN]. It's for you.

> [*He hands over the horn, still attached to him by its cord.*]

GAWAIN. Och, she's been chasing me from Hallowe'en to Hogmanay!

> [*He embarks on a conversation with the twitter that emerges from the horn.*]

Hallo, mother. Look, must you track me everywhere I go? I'm sorry. I didn't mean to be impertinent. What? I've *always* answered. Three days ago? Well, yes, I did hear you, but—yes, I was spending the night in the wood. Alone! I couldn't reply. There was a wolf eating my supper. A *wolf,* mother! No, I didn't, not after he'd been mumbling it over. Of course I've eaten since. I'm staying with friends. No, you don't know them. Well, I have *some.*

> [*He looks at the others helplessly. They give him kindly smiles.*]

Mother, I am not playing the fool! The king sent me on a—an errand of state. No, I *haven't* been thrown out! I'm sorry, mother. I didn't mean to shout. It's a secret. Of course, it's not a plot against you! Oh, mother, I can't tell you! I'm not sly and secretive. Oh, if you must know—it began with a riddle, mother. The king——

> [BERCILAK *takes the horn away from him, and speaks to it himself.*]

BERCILAK. You've been disconnected, madam. [*To* GAWAIN] You shouldn't worry her surely, with details of this quest?

> [GAWAIN *suddenly looks shaken and faint.* BERCILAK *steadies him.*]

GAWAIN. She holds me on a leash—like a puppy-dog! I—feel odd!

> [*He looks at* MIRIEL.]

But you drank that wine, too.

MIRIEL. Not from the same cup.

> [BERCILAK *lowers* GAWAIN *on to the couch, and pulls the rug over him.* MIRIEL *moves downstage.* BERCILAK *goes to her, stretching out his hand.*]

BERCILAK. The night has fallen.

MIRIEL. No!

> [*She runs from the room.* BERCILAK *glances at* GAWAIN, *who is asleep.*]

BERCILAK. Playing with fire, who knows which hand may singe?

> [*He goes out, and the room darkens. The tapestries wave in the flickering lights. The horn sounds its faraway music. The voice speaks through it:*]

VOICE. Playing with fire—with fire—and time passing and passing——

> [GAWAIN *gives a cry, and jumps to his feet. The room becomes silent and still. Light returns to that of evening. He speaks distractedly:*]

GAWAIN. Leave your watching and your shadowing!

> [*The door opens.* MIRIEL *is just outside.*]

Leave me alone!

> [*He catches his breath, and backs away from her.*]

Oh, but you're not she!

> [MIRIEL *comes further into the room. She has changed again. She looks wiser, more mature. She has a dull-gold circlet round her head, with green stones set in it, and a green silk ribbon*]

> *round her waist, embroidered with golden*
> *flowers. She might be playing a Witch, but a*
> *kind one.* GAWAIN *hardly seems to notice her.*]

MIRIEL. For what nightmare do you take me?

GAWAIN [*Unsteadily*]. I have dreamed of witchcraft—and
of death. Her eyes were watching—staring—everywhere——!

MIRIEL. Someone you know?

GAWAIN. All my life.

> [*He pulls himself together, and now says very*
> *politely:*]

I'm sorry to offer you so poor a welcome, madam. But,
if you've brought food or drink, I don't think I——

MIRIEL. Look. Empty-handed. Today, you'll feast with us.
If it eases your mind, everything shall be tasted before
you touch it.

GAWAIN. Tonight I must go to the Green Chapel. My
chances there may be less—less doubtful—if I'm not
drugged half-conscious.

MIRIEL. No drug, I promise. Your hands are shaking.
Those were bad dreams you had.

> [*He nods. She is being very gentle, and he reacts*
> *instinctively. Perhaps he has dreamed in the past*
> *of a kind mother.*]

Come and sit down. Oh, don't be afraid of me. I won't
hurt you. I am quite gentle. Quite harmless.

GAWAIN. So are the grasses that conceal a trap.

MIRIEL. That's unkind.

GAWAIN. My unwary tongue!

MIRIEL. You—unwary?

> [*He has gone to sit by the window, and she*

[77]

> *circles round the room, considering her next move.*]

You understand very little about women.

GAWAIN. The High Queen threw a few maidens in our way from time to time, like honey-cakes to good children. They were tedious.

MIRIEL. As I said, you understand little about women. You fear them all, for your mother's sake. Do you not?

> [*He says nothing to this, and she goes on very kindly:*]

I think you do. Poor Gawain. Tell me something.

GAWAIN. Whatever you ask, my lady.

MIRIEL. Why won't you say you love me?

> [*He is startled into wariness, and begins to think.*]

GAWAIN. Well—because—well, I will say so.

MIRIEL. You will?

GAWAIN. It would be unmannerly *not* to love my gracious hostess—and Sir Bercilak, too. I mean, I have the utmost affection for you both.

MIRIEL. Lord of light! How you twist and turn! I don't know what my husband hunts today, but, if it's as foxy as you, he'll come back empty-handed!

> [*She goes quickly to him, grabs him by one shoulder, and turns him to face her.*]

GAWAIN. Mind my arm!

MIRIEL. I'm not touching it. It's the other one! Look into my eyes. Don't dare turn away. Tell me truly— do you love some other lady? And I don't mean your beastly mother!

GAWAIN. Well——

MIRIEL. The truth, Gawain!

GAWAIN. I love no lady. Nor do I ever wish to.

> [*She stares at him hard. Then she releases him and moves away.*]

MIRIEL. I am truly answered. And to my true sorrow.

GAWAIN [*Plaintively*]. You cornered me.

MIRIEL. Poor Gawain.

> [*She stoops over his upturned head, and kisses him gently on the mouth.*]

And that's the last of your ransom.

> [*She moves towards the door. He rises, looking greatly relieved. And she pauses, and says without turning:*]

Would you—would you grant me one small favour?

GAWAIN. If possible, madam.

MIRIEL. I'd like a token—a keepsake. Will you give me one of your gloves?

> [*He looks at her thoughtfully. A pause.*]

GAWAIN. I think not. Scuffed leather and rusty metal makes a mean gift. If I had something of value—but I brought no trinkets on this journey. Bercilak would think poorly of me, if I dishonoured your hospitality with a shabby keepsake. My gratitude must serve as payment.

MIRIEL. Distrustful as ever, my hero! Very well, I'll give you a gift.

GAWAIN. Having nothing to offer, I can accept nothing.

MIRIEL. Something valueless?

> [*She replaces the ring, and unties the green ribbon from about her waist.*]

A silk ribbon, embroidered with flowers.

> [*She offers it on her outstretched hand. He shakes his head. She sighs, and crumples the silk in her fingers.*]

Very well. And yet I've heard it said that such a ribbon could save a man's life. Green silk, and golden flowers. It could save him from harm, no matter how he adventured.

> [*She looks at him, with a level and penetrating gaze. He shifts uneasily.*]

It may be just a foolish tale. Or—it might be true.

> [*She pauses.* GAWAIN *stares at the ribbon she is coiling through her hands.*]

For instance, if you have any cause to fear whatever you meet tonight——

> [*She pauses again. He draws a ragged breath.*]

GAWAIN [*Slowly*]. I have a little fear in me.

MIRIEL. With this, you might also have a little hope. Handled rightly, the ribbon may keep hurt from you. May, not will—there is no promise.

> [*She puts the ribbon on the table, and turns away. Against his better judgement, he is drawn to it. She turns to watch him. He takes up the ribbon. Behind his back, she makes a sudden movement as though to prevent him. Then she covers her mouth with her hands and stays still.*]

GAWAIN. I thank you, Lady Miriel.

MIRIEL. Oh—wait. Before you—accept it—I must ask you to keep the gift secret. My husband must not know.

[*A pause.* GAWAIN *sees a crooked path opening before him.*]

Can you make that promise?

[*Another pause. Here is, in fact, the moment of truth.* GAWAIN *realises it. But he looks at the ribbon, hesitates, and sets his foot on the path.*]

GAWAIN [*Under his breath*]. I promise.

[*The hunting-horn sounds.*]

MIRIEL. Be careful, Gawain. Oh, do be careful.

[*The door opens.* BERCILAK *is standing on the threshold.* MIRIEL *starts, but makes no move towards him.*]

Ah! How went *your* hunting?

BERCILAK. Not worth the winning!

[*He strides into the room. He surveys* GAWAIN *for a moment, rather sombrely. There is a change in* BERCILAK. *Some of his heartiness is missing, and he is sterner and colder. In fact, he is not enjoying the current situation as much as he thought he would.*]

Will you be first, this time, to pay our score?

GAWAIN. If you wish.

BERCILAK. So far, Orkney, you have played fair. What do you owe me now?

GAWAIN. This.

[*He kisses* BERCILAK'S *hand, and lays the hand against its owner's lips.*]

BERCILAK [*Gravely*]. You had sweet fortune, sir. And was this all?

GAWAIN [*Avoiding his eye*]. That's all I have to offer you.

BERCILAK. And this is all I have to offer *you!*

[81]

[He tosses a somewhat battered fox-skin on the ground at GAWAIN'S *feet.]*

A fox!

[He moves away. He goes on speaking in a bleak voice.]

I had hoped, sir, for something worthy of you. The day began in hope, but ends in shame. I hunt for food. Not to worry small creatures to their misery and destruction. That's no work for any but a bully. This fool of an animal crossed our path. My hounds could not be recalled. Even then he might have escaped—he almost did, the cunning one—but he thought himself too clever and doubled once too often. And there he is. All his brightness torn and stained. All his pride destroyed.

MIRIEL. Poor fox.

BERCILAK [*To* GAWAIN]. And you, sir—your time is running short. I would keep you here in safety, if I could. But my word was given to show you the place you must find tonight. And I do not break my word.

GAWAIN [*Unhappily*]. If you'd just explain the path I have to follow——

BERCILAK. I meant to guide you myself. But I can do better. I'll send someone who is well known to you. He's being instructed now.

GAWAIN. Who is it?

BERCILAK. Don't spoil my last gift to you. You'll know who it is, when the time comes, and be glad of his company. Your armour is sanded, and all your gear made ready. The great horse is being dressed in his trappings. I'll act as your squire and arm you, later. Meanwhile, come and eat with us.

GAWAIN. Bercilak, I—I——

[*A slight pause. They look at him closely.*]
I have no words to thank you.

      [MIRIEL *comes to his other side. She speaks very sadly.*]

MIRIEL. May all the gods you know go with you, Gawain.

BERCILAK. We have only this comfort to offer, now—take both our hearts on your journey towards midnight.

CURTAIN

A MOUNTAIN-SIDE AT MIDNIGHT

Everything is very dark, streaked through with long bright shafts of moonlight. There is an open sky at the back, and mists are blowing over. Down left and right are clumps of tall, bare, black trees. Up right stand two twisted thorn-bushes, with their tops interlocked as though they formed the gateway to some unseen place beyond. On each of their stems is nailed the white skull of a sheep. Snow lies everywhere, and a wind is shrilly singing.

[84]

GAWAIN *comes in from down right. He wears his chain-mail, but no helmet, and the metal hood is lying back on his shoulders.* MIRIEL'S *green ribbon is wound round his left shoulder, under his plaid.* GAHERIS *is with him. They are quarrelling.*

GAWAIN. Well, it was a pretty funny thing to do!

GAHERIS. It was not so funny, wondering all these long months just what daft scrapes you were getting into! Uncle Arthur was half out of his mind. So was I.

GAWAIN. When were you ever in it? You knew I must make this search alone. What possessed you to follow?

GAHERIS. You did make it alone! I followed far behind. Asking people if they'd seen——

GAWAIN. The Green Knight bade me come alone.

GAHERIS. So you will, Gawain. I'm following no further. The Green Chapel is up there, behind yon thorns.

GAWAIN. Wait for me at the foot of the hill. If I don't come in an hour, see to Gringolet.

GAHERIS. The king has gone back to Narberth in Wales. All this year, there has been fighting over the whole country. He badly wants you back. Go to him now. Not up there. You haven't a chance. Your death is waiting there, and you know it.

GAWAIN. I've no choice, have I?

GAHERIS. Well, now, I've been thinking——

GAWAIN. Don't tell me!

[GAHERIS *goes and catches him by the arm.*]

GAHERIS. You're acting like a fool! I heard more of this Green Knight from Sir Bercilak's people, and he's

[85]

a terrible cruel creature. None who comes near his lair escapes the axe. Man, if you had twenty lives, he'd take them all.

GAWAIN. You cheer me.

GAHERIS. Don't make a jest of it!

GAWAIN. What should I do? Cling round your neck and whimper?

GAHERIS. Just come away. For pity's sake—how shall I feel, to watch you go alone to your death!

GAWAIN. Don't look.

[*Then he speaks more kindly.*]

Don't fret yourself so. It may be—there's just a chance for me. You go back to the horses, and forbye we'll yet ride to Wales together. I meant none of my scolding. You know I've a wicked tongue, and a vile bad temper. It's not so easy to send you away, mo chridhe——

GAHERIS. But I was thinking, Gawain—and don't go gibing at me——!

GAWAIN. No, no! Of course you can think a little.

GAHERIS. If you come with me now, and not go near that place—we'll tell everyone you met the Knight, and that he spared your life. No wait! *You* need not speak of it at all. I'll do it. I'll swear by my soul and my sword, and everything that's sacred, that I stood by and saw what happened. He was merciful and let you go scatheless. No one will ever know you turned back.

[*A slight pause. Then* GAWAIN *speaks slowly and with some difficulty.*]

GAWAIN. You've known me all your life, brother. Over thirty years. Is that your judgement of me? I never thought to look at myself through your eyes, and see a crawling coward! Go on! Go on standing there, and telling me how cheap you hold me. If you want to make me glad of death, you must be satisfied now.

[*He turns away.*]

I've no high opinion of myself, and never had—but at least I tried for courage. Of some sort!

GAHERIS. I'm sorry! I'm sorry! It was my own cowardice speaking. I just don't want you killed. Forget what I said. I'm a fool!

GAWAIN. Gaheris——

[*He half-turns to the other.*]

I'll not part from you in anger. You've always minded me. You've been a fine brother to me. Just—don't say any more, will you! Go away now.

[GAHERIS *tries to say something and fails. He starts to go off down right.* GAWAIN *swings round to him.*]

Ah, wait a moment!

[*He goes to his brother, and gives him a brief hug.* GAHERIS *goes blindly off, down right.* GAWAIN *watches him go. Then he rubs a hand across his face, and unbuckles his sword-sling. He moves upstage and sees the sheep skulls. He crosses and looks between the thorn-bushes. He does not like what he sees there. Then a sound makes him spin round quickly. It is the sound of an axe being sharpened, somewhere*] *out of sight to the left.* GAWAIN *listens for a few moments. His nerve cracks slightly, and he gulps and puts a hand to his throat. He calls loudly:*]

If that's your greeting to me, you've made your effect! Now show yourself, if you're the one I've come to meet. This is Gawain of Orkney.

[*The noise continues.* GAWAIN *moves forward a little.*]

It's a cold place here, to stand waiting—and listening. And unmannerly in you to keep me so. It's close on midnight. I've kept my word. Are you for breaking yours?

[*The honing stops. Through the mist, the* GREEN KNIGHT *comes striding. His head is back on his neck, and he comes to a halt and looks at* GAWAIN *with glowing red eyes. A pause.* GAWAIN, *with an effort, goes on speaking.*]

I—don't care over much for your Chapel. A hollow barrow—a grave-mound. Only fitted for unholy rites. And a bitter wind blowing from it. Do you mean to make me go in there?

KNIGHT. This open ground will serve. Welcome, sir. I trust you recollect the purpose of our meeting?

GAWAIN. It's not a thing that slips the memory.

[*The* KNIGHT *runs his thumb down the blade of the axe.*]

KNIGHT. Come, then. This mist may blunt the blade. Finish the game now.

GAWAIN. As quickly as you will.

[88]

[*He leans his sword against a tree, and goes towards the* KNIGHT, *pushing back his mail hood from his neck.*]

KNIGHT. No need for that, sir. My axe will cut through armour as swiftly as it slices flesh and bone. One blow is all my due, and——

GAWAIN. And one will suffice.

[*He is about to kneel, when a thin whistling comes from one of the sheep-skulls.*]

I'm not answering that!

KNIGHT. Not even to say farewell?

[GAWAIN *hesitates. Then he goes to the skull, and speaks close to it, with miserable anger. It twitters in reply a few times.*]

GAWAIN. It's Gawain, and I don't want to talk just now. Oh, I'm sorry, then! But I—mother, I'm busy. Just for once, will you leave me alone! I am not living a life of dissolute pleasure! Mother, I'm in a bit of a hurry. I—mother, could you not for once just say good-bye, in a kind sort of way? Yes, maybe I am absurd, but——

[*The twittering stops abruptly.* GAWAIN *looks at the skull bitterly.*]

Och, she might have—just this time——

[*He breaks off, and stalks back to the* KNIGHT.]

I hope you had a human mother, sir!

KNIGHT. Well——

[*But* GAWAIN *has not realised the implication of what he has said. He kneels, in a rage of hurt dignity.*]

III. i

GAWAIN. Take your blow, and let me be done with it all.

> [*The* KNIGHT *slowly lifts the axe above his shoulder, and* GAWAIN *bends his head.*]

KNIGHT. I will take only my right, sir.

> [*He brings the axe down fast, but stops just before he touches* GAWAIN, *who has jerked his head aside. The* KNIGHT *speaks with grave reproach.*]

You flinched with fear before you felt the stroke. I never did so, when I knelt for yours.

GAWAIN. My head is not replaceable. I should not have moved, and will not do so again. Finish it now!

> [*Again the* KNIGHT *swings up the axe, and again as it descends, he halts the blow.* GAWAIN *looks up at him crossly.*]

Why do you hesitate?

KNIGHT. To see if you stayed still.

GAWAIN. I did so! You dawdle overlong. I might die of boredom!

KNIGHT. Not you, Gawain.

> [*He swings his axe a third time. He halts it, and then drops it on* GAWAIN'S *neck, just hard enough to wound him slightly. The* KNIGHT *raises the axe, and waits, with the haft resting across his shoulder. After feeling the blow,* GAWAIN *puts a hand to the back of his neck, looks at the blood on his fingers, and jumps to his feet. He backs to the thorn-bush and takes up his sword.*]

GAWAIN. You've taken your return stroke. If you want more, I'm not called on to submit unresisting.

> [*The* KNIGHT *leans on his axe, and laughs.*]

KNIGHT. Sheath your sword. I've no quarrel with you, sir. If I wished to see your head on the ground, I could have put it there.

GAWAIN. Why didn't you?

KNIGHT. Measure for measure Gawain. At my castle, for three days you played fairly, giving me the prizes that you won. I held back the first axe-stroke— not only because you shrank from it, but for my wife's kiss that you repaid to me. The second for the second. And the third——

GAWAIN [*Under his breath*]. You are Bercilak?

KNIGHT. The people of the Hills have many shapes. Even the third blow was not struck to kill. If I could, I would have spared you that small wound. We tested you in many ways, and almost you won through in perfect honour. But—somewhat you flagged, sir. In just one thing you failed. And the green ribbon on your shoulder cost you the gash you bear.

> [*Understanding*, GAWAIN *finds the knowledge bitter. He pulls off the ribbon, and drops it on the ground.*]

Too late, Orkney.

GAWAIN. All the time—you waited all the time for me to lie to you. And at the last, I lied.

KNIGHT. For fear of death. A less worthy lie would have cost you your head. There is no power at all in that ribbon. It was only part of a test.

GAWAIN. I've done well. I kept the ribbon from you. I couldn't bide the fall of the axe. There's nothing to say. Let me go now.

III. i

KNIGHT. Try to forgive me and yourself.

GAWAIN. I'm not a forgiving person. Now—my brother will be waiting——

KNIGHT. He is not.

GAWAIN [*Not heeding this remark*]. And the king—the king will be wanting to hear how my journeying ended.

> [*He starts to move down right, and suddenly stops, and looks at the other.*]

Why did you do it? I took your challenge. Couldn't you be content to strike your proper blow?

KNIGHT. Orkney, I have been under enchantment. Unless a man was bold enough to submit to the axe—and honest enough to escape with his life—I must have kept this guise from time to time, forever. Be content with your victory in this, at least.

> [GAWAIN *goes and picks up the ribbon.*]

GAWAIN. You said I could keep this. So I will. And wear it always, plain to see. To remind me. For fear I might deceive myself into some pride again.

> [*He turns away, and pauses as the* KNIGHT'S *next words halt him.*]

KNIGHT. What are you going to do?

GAWAIN. Return to the king. Tell him—and everyone— what I've done here. If they also make excuses for me, I know fine where I can go to hear the truth. Where I'd thought never to run again!

KNIGHT. You mean to pull your whole life down about your head?

> [GAWAIN *goes to the trees, down right, and pauses. He says, without turning and without emotion:*]

GAWAIN. Thank you for your hospitality. Commend me to your lady.

> [*He goes out. The* KNIGHT *stands with hands folded on the head of the axe, looking after him.*]

KNIGHT. A frame of mind to lose everything for us all. But spur as fast as you may, my friend, I know another road.

CURTAIN

THE QUEEN'S DRESSING-ROOM
AT NARBERTH

*Only a small corner of this room can be seen. At the back
is a hanging tapestry. Down centre left is a table, and a
stool. There are various oddments on the table, jewels,
ornaments, make-up, and such.*

RAGNELL *sits on the stool, looking at her hideous little
face in a hand-mirror of polished metal. The* QUEEN
stands near, watching her with troubled eyes.

QUEEN. Ragnell, try wearing one ear-ring only. It might
balance the—the effect.

[RAGNELL *removes one of her ear-rings, and looks at the* QUEEN *patiently.*]

Yes, I'm sure that's better. Don't you think so?

RAGNELL. I think the beauty of your jewels is mocked, without improving mine.

QUEEN. You're not to talk like that. We have to do the best we can with the—the means at our disposal.

[RAGNELL *gives a sad little laugh. She looks into the mirror again, and then covers her face with her free hand. The* QUEEN *goes to her side.*]

Poor child! It isn't fair!

[*She becomes business-like again. She takes a jewelled circlet from the table, and places it on* RAGNELL'S *head.*]

Ragnell, since you came back two days ago, I've grown to like you. I'm not going to treat you like a fool, and pretend you have an easy face to organise. But it would be very boring if every woman had the beauty of Dierdre.

RAGNELL. I'd gladly settle for ordinary plainness.

[*She gets up, and goes to the* QUEEN *and takes her hand.*]

You've been very kind to me, madam. Kinder than I thought a human could ever be. Oh, your ladies—and all the returned knights—they try hard to hide their pity, and their revulsion, but——

QUEEN. When they know you better, they'll like you for yourself, and then——

RAGNELL. Yes, people can grow fond of apes.

QUEEN. Ragnell, no! You mustn't think like that.

RAGNELL. Look—look here!

[*She picks up the mirror again, and holds it so*

> *that her face and the face of the* QUEEN *are reflected together.*]

The face of the Queen of Britain—and the face of the future Queen!

QUEEN [*Turning away*]. Mine is a face of practised royalty. The one I wear when I'm alone may not be what you see.

RAGNELL. I can't go through with this. If Gawain returns, I'll free him from his vow.

QUEEN. That isn't in your power, my dear. The promise was made to give Arthur his year for finding the riddle's answer. He has had the year, and the promise must be kept.

RAGNELL. But has he found the answer?

QUEEN. He's written down all the guesses everyone has made. When the Green Knight comes, he will be shown the list. Whatever the result, Gawain's word must stand. There will be a wedding. Now, I wonder—could you wear a veil over——?

RAGNELL. Oh, let us play fair! Let the world see the price that's being paid by—whoever marries me. It's the least I can do.

> [*She hesitates, and then says in a very small voice:*]

How long does a wedding take?

QUEEN. It would be worse in the capital. Here it will only be a family affair. Yet, even so—it will seem long to you.

RAGNELL. All those eyes watching! And the hand of my husband shuddering away from mine. But—it will be over at last—and I can go back to my own place.

QUEEN. Will your—husband—just let you go?

RAGNELL [*With a desolate small laugh*]. Will he beg me to stay?

> [*A pause. The* QUEEN *takes a jar from the table, and a hare's foot.*]

QUEEN. The future guards its secrets well. Let me see if a touch of rouge on one side would help to—help to—to——

RAGNELL. Experiment as you please, madam. It won't make matters worse.

> [*She sits at the table, and shuts her eyes. The* QUEEN *dabbles the hare's-foot in the jar, and considers what to do next. From a distance comes the sound of a hunting-horn. The two women start, and look at one another in uneasy surmise.*]

CURTAIN

THE PARLOUR AT NARBERTH. THE SAME EVENING

The room is only lit by the flicker of flame from the fire, and moonlight through the window, down left. The chessmen are on the table, as in Act One, Scene One. From some distance away beyond the closed door, can be heard the murmur of voices from a considerable gathering of people, there is also an uncoordinated cheer, and some laughter. The door opens, admitting louder noise and GAWAIN. *He shuts the door behind him, and the voices fade to a murmur again.*

He leans against the door for a moment, then he goes towards the table, in a blind sort of way. He bangs one fist on it, making the chess-men dance, then goes to the fireplace, and leans his head on his hands against the stones. He stays still for a while, then, hearing someone

[98]

*at the door, he moves quickly down right, and into the
shadow of the hanging tapestry there.* KAY *comes into
the room. He looks all round, and speaks tentatively.*

KAY. Gawain?

> [*Getting no reply, and seeing no one there, he
> speaks over his shoulder to the corridor outside.*]

He's not here.

> [*The* KING *enters quietly.*]

Shall I have a look in his own quarters?

KING. You do that, Kay. And look in the stables and
kitchens.

KAY. What on earth would he be doing there?

KING [*Vaguely*]. Well, I don't know. Patting the horses——

KAY. Do you quite understand your nephew?

KING. I like to think so.

KAY. Beyond me! What made him bolt like that? He told
his story quite calmly—and running himself down for
no reason anyone could see—waited to see how it was
taken, and when they all cheered him, he chucked his
sword on the floor, and fled. Why?

KING. Perhaps because they cheered.

KAY. Is he entirely deranged?

KING. Ask him when you find him.

KAY. And get my hand bitten? Oh well—I'd better have
a good look in the attics, among the bats!

> [*He goes out. The* KING *closes the door.*]

KING. Gawain, I know you're here.

> [*He gets no reply, and tries again.*]

I'll go away if you want me to, but I'd rather not.

> [*No reply. The* KING *takes a pace or two forward
> towards the fire.*]

[99]

Well? Shall I leave you alone?

GAWAIN [*From the shadow.*] I can't order you to go.

KING. No. But you can ask.

> [*A pause. He goes and sits in the chair by the fire.*]

I'd just like to tell you something. May I? And don't say you can't stop me, because you know you can.

> [*Silence. He holds out his hands to the fire, and goes on speaking quietly.*]

It's galling when people think more highly of you than you do of yourself. If you feel guilty, you want to lie down and be kicked. That pays you out and you lose the guilt. If no one kicks, the guilt remains. And if you're praised, instead—cheered loudly for reasons you think false, then the obvious thing is to run away and hide.

GAWAIN. How do you know? Have you ever——?

KING. Oh, come, come, Gawain! Most of us have something that weighs on our souls like under-done suet pudding. Couldn't you come out from under the rug, or wherever you are?

GAWAIN. If you insist.

KING. No, I don't insist. I'd rather talk to you than to thin air. But if you prefer to go on lurking—lurk.

> [GAWAIN *emerges unwillingly from his lurking-place.*]

That's much better. You can't go through life draped in an arras. It's cosy, but not constructive. Come and sit down—here.

> [*He indicates the stool downstage of the fireplace.* GAWAIN *goes and sits on this, keeping his head lowered and averted from his uncle.*]

Was that so hard to do?

GAWAIN. You make it seem easy, but——

KING. Yes, the rest of the world must be faced, too.

GAWAIN. No!

KING. Where will you run next?

> [*A slight pause.*]

Fifteen years ago, when you were censured for things that hadn't bothered you much, you ran way. Just from sheer pride and temper. It would take some fortitude to stay here now, and face the approval that you don't entirely deserve.

GAWAIN. I'm not brave. I've proved it.

KING. No one else——

GAWAIN. No one else seems to have any judgement! I told you what I did. I told everyone. There was no honour in any of it! And they—applauded!

KING. Go on.

GAWAIN. All that nonsense with Lady Miriel was nothing. A game. Why would I want her? What sort of tests were those? But this one——

> [*He touches the knot of green ribbon on his shoulder and glances at the door.*]

They laughed about this. A detail, they said! And they'll wear a knot of green ribbon in my honour! Arthur, *you* don't think it a detail?

KING. It wasn't very good, Gawain.

GAWAIN. And I turned from the axe.

KING. Most men would.

GAWAIN. But *I* did! I've left myself without a shred of honour. How am I going to live?

KING. Keeping your views to yourself. Letting people admire your courage and chivalry. It will be good for them.

GAWAIN. Huh!

KING [*Patientl*]. No, not 'huh''. If you're determined to do penance, wear this one like a hair-shirt. Irksome, but reputedly good for the soul.

GAWAIN. Well, I won't!

KING. Don't snap at me, Gawain.

> [GAWAIN *gives an exclamation, and goes to kneel by the* KING.]

GAWAIN. I've let you down again.

KING. I need you badly, you know. When I sent for you last year, I sent for help. It's too much responsibility for one man to carry alone.

GAWAIN. But I'm not——

KING. You won that fight for me, three months ago, at Lindum. If you hadn't turned the Saxons on the flank—

GAWAIN. How did you——?

KING. I'm not half-witted. I know my men, even with blank shields. No one else goes quite berserk! And you can lead.

GAWAIN. Not lacking all respect for myself——

KING. Yes, well—think about someone else for a moment, will you? The Lady Ragnell has been asking to say good-bye to you.

GAWAIN. I don't want to see her. I married her this morning. Now she can go back to her brother. Your year is paid for.

KING. You feel no sort of pity for her?

GAWAIN. She's part of all this mess of sorcery!

> [*There is a single, thunderous knock on the door.* GAWAIN *looks hunted.*]

I won't speak to anyone!

KING. It might just possibly be someone to speak to *me*. I'll send them away, but see who it is.

> [*There is another knock.* GAWAIN *hesitates.*]

Open the door, Gawain.

> [*A third and louder knock. The* KING *rises.*]

Or get out of the way and let me do it.

> [GAWAIN *goes and opens the door. Outside stands a tall and sinister figure. A man in a great black cloak, black chain-mail, a black metal helmet, mailed gauntlets, and a black surcoat blazoned with gleaming green symbols. His eyes gleam greenly, too. His beard is pale golden. He is splendid and terrible and royal, for this is a Prince of the Sidhe in his own shape. His name is* KYNAN. *All round him a white mist is blowing. If* GAWAIN *is impressed, the only sign is the sudden straightening of his back. The* KING *stays calm.*]

GAWAIN. What do you want?

> [KYNAN *advances slowly, and* GAWAIN'S *hand gropes for his missing sword.*]

KYNAN. Stand aside, Orkney. My word is for the king.

> [GAWAIN *moves between him and the* KING, *and Arthur puts him to one side.*]

KING. Since you come here unannounced, and yet a stranger, I take it you are no ordinary knight.

KYNAN. I am Kynan Ban, Prince of the Eildon Hills. In my rightful shape and being. I am also known by other names—the Green Knight—Bercilak——

> [GAWAIN *gives a choked exclamation, and moves away to the left. He stands with his back to the room, pretending not to be there.*]

Your—champion—is easily quelled.

KING. By those names, are you surprised? You've come for the sword?

KYNAN. Not quite yet.

KING. The year has been a troubled one. Yet I've tried to find the answer to your riddle. I made a list——

KYNAN. I've seen it. No answer is correct.

KING. How did you see it?

KYNAN. I have means. All day I've been here at your castle. I watched the wedding of my sister and your heir.

KING. I didn't notice you.

KYNAN. I have means to ensure that, also.

KING. Yes, you would. So—by right, you are part of my family, now. Welcome, whatever darker reasons bring you here. How long is left for me to find the answer?

KYNAN. It doesn't lie with you, sir, and never did. It is so arranged that only one person can tell you the answer. And one other can make that telling possible. The matter is out of your hands, and mine. The last chance lies now with one man.

> [*He looks at* GAWAIN. *The* KING'S *eyes follow his.*]

KING. No. Nothing more will be laid on him. Prince, I speak as King of Britain. From one world to another, in equal authority. Take the sword. We'll do without it. Leave us to recover as best we may from the touch of darkness.

KYNAN. I hoped for another ending. I have no wish to take your sword. Nor to destroy him. At the start— but not now. I know him now. I set him a series of jumps. And he took them, with a couple of small stumbles. Now, with the finish in sight, comes the most difficult barrier of all. If that's refused or failed, everyone will suffer. You, my sister, myself, and——

> [*Again his gaze rests on* GAWAIN. *Then he turns to the* KING.]

Give me your leave to try him. You've applied sweet reason. Let me throw in pride.

KING [*Slowly*]. God help him, if I lay him open to further hurt, but—you have my leave.

KYNAN [*Compellingly*]. Orkney!

> [*There is no response. The* KING *watches gravely and anxiously.*]

Turn and face me, Orkney.

GAWAIN [*Unmoving*]. I refuse your jump.

KYNAN. You don't even know what it is.

> [*A pause.*]

I challenge you! To no ordinary fight. If pride won't spur you, will anger be the rowel?

> [*He peels off a glove, and flicks* GAWAIN *lightly on the shoulder with it. The other man turns like a cat.* KYNAN *tosses the glove on the floor between them.* GAWAIN *makes a move towards it, but draws back at the last moment.*]

GAWAIN. And I refuse your challenge.

KYNAN. I never thought to hear that from Gawain.

GAWAIN. It's a fine new experience for you. You'll not make me lose my temper, say what you will.

> [*The loss is not so far off, though. He turns away to hide the fact.*]

KYNAN. You're only keeping it from sheer bad temper!

GAWAIN. Leave me alone.

III. iii

> [*The door opens suddenly, and* KAY *comes in with* GAHERIS.]

KAY. We can't find him anywhere—oh, you've got him!

GAHERIS. Gawain.

> [*Ignoring everyone else, he goes to his brother, and catches his arm.* GAWAIN *shakes him off angrily, and turns his back on him.*]

What's the matter with you? All day you've refused me a word or a look—ever since you came back. What have I done?

> [*Getting no reply, his own temper begins to rise.*]

I'll not be so treated by you!

> [KYNAN *takes a pace towards them, but the* KING *halts him.*]

KING [*Quietly*]. Perhaps a good family row——?

GAHERIS. I've a right to know my fault.

GAWAIN. You know it.

GAHERIS. I'm not a mind-reader!

> [GAWAIN *turns on him at last, and speaks with gathering fury.*]

GAWAIN. You heard me tell them what happened when I met—that one—on the hill. But I never named your name. I held it secret, to save your face!

GAHERIS. How did *I* get into it?

> [*The family row is well under way.* KYNAN *and the* KING *are listening and watching intently.*]

GAWAIN. What sort of a bribe did you take from Bercilak? For using our old love and trust to trip me?

GAHERIS. Are you mad!

KAY. Here we go.

> [GAHERIS *grabs his brother, and glares at him.*]

[106]

GAHERIS. Stop your twisted talk!

> [*He is thrown off, violently. The brothers are almost at fighting point.*]

GAWAIN. Fine straight speaking I had from you by the death-mound! *And* you rode off without waiting. I'd have had it out with you, then—and told no one of your treachery——

KYNAN. Gawain!

KING. Don't stop them.

KYNAN. Fuel to the flame. Gawain, your brother did no wrong to you.

GAWAIN. Only carried out your orders to make me break my tryst. To talk me into hiding behind lies—to lose the little honour I had left!

GAHERIS. Did I so! I would maybe have knocked you on your addled head, and gone under the axe in your place—but I wasn't there! I was not there! Take back your lies, Gawain, or I'll—no, I can't hit you, even now. But I'll never see you again.

KYNAN. Gawain, it was not he who took you to the Green Chapel, but another in his shape.

> [*There is a stricken pause.*]

GAWAIN [*Slowly*]. It was you.

KYNAN. My pretence of brotherly concern blunted your judgement.

> [GAWAIN *makes a sudden move as though to snatch up the gauntlet from the floor.* KYNAN *and the* KING *look hopeful. But, again,* GAWAIN *draws back.*]

GAWAIN. You left out nothing, did you!

> [*He goes away from everyone, down left.*]

[107]

III. iii

KAY [*Quite baffled*]. What are you all doing to him?

KING. Not much good, so far.

KYNAN. There's one move left. An unsure one. But if that fails, we're all in great trouble.

> [*He gestures towards the door with one hand. After a moment,* RAGNELL *comes into the room. The* KING *looks from her to* GAWAIN.]

KING. A faint chance. Kay—Gaheris—come with me, please.

> [*He collects* KAY *and* KYNAN, *and takes them to the door. But* GAHERIS *hovers by his brother, who suddenly notices him, and clutches his sleeve.*]

GAWAIN. They twisted my mind in spirals, Gaheris. I'm sorry. Of course you wouldn't——! Gaheris, stay with the king. He'll be needing an heir, now. And there'll be trouble with Scotland, if he hasn't got one of us.

GAHERIS. Where are you going, then?

GAWAIN. Back where I belong.

GAHERIS. No!

KING. Gaheris.

> [GAHERIS *casts a dazed look from his brother to the* KING, *and goes unwillingly to the latter.*]

GAHERIS. I go home with him, if he goes!

KING. I don't doubt it.

> [*He removes* GAHERIS, KAY, *and* KYNAN *from the room. A pause.*]

RAGNELL. All the ways are parting. They said you wouldn't let me take my leave of you, nor even see you. But here I am to say farewell.

> [*At the sound of her voice,* GAWAIN *starts, not*

knowing she is in the room. Now he speaks
politely and coldly, without turning.]

GAWAIN. A safe journey to you, Lady Ragnell.

> [*She turns to the door, hesitates, and looks back*
> *at him.*]

RAGNELL. I meant to depart on that note of dignity. But
I must tell you this—you brought it all on yourself, you
know. You didn't *have* to behead the Green Knight.
But we knew you would.

GAWAIN. Yes, I've a fine reputation for beheading people!
Mostly women, of course.

RAGNELL. You've a fine reputation for going out of your
mind when anyone you love is hurt!

> [*Without realising it, these two are embarked*
> *on another sort of family row.*]

We laid the riddle on the king, knowing you'd swear
to marry me, to give him his year—*and* lose your
temper with the Knight, as a result. It was you we aimed
for, all the time. The traps were set for you. Not for the
king.

GAWAIN [*Half turning to her*]. Why *me?*

RAGNELL. Because your dread lady-mother had dealings
with the Hollow Hills, and began a feud with Kynan.
He is too powerful to be hurt by any mortal—even a
witch—so she struck at me instead, and made me—
what you see.

> [GAWAIN *turns at last. He listens to what she is*
> *saying, with deep interest.*]

We meant to even the score through you. Your dishonour if you refused the tests—your death by the axe
if you failed them. You were only the son of Morgawse
to us, then. And now, we've all lost. The sword will
vanish. I must stay as I am for keeps. And you're

running back to her like a beaten dog, so that she can crow her head off over the lot of us!

GAWAIN [*Half knowing the answer*]. And the harmless people that were killed at the Green Chapel? What had *they* done to you?

RAGNELL. Don't be *stupid*, Gawain! There is no Green Chapel. An illusion—even Bercilak's castle was an illusion. The axe never hurt anyone.

> [*He touches the back of his neck, with an angry scowl at her.*]

GAWAIN. Only me. Dia! Because I told a bit of a lie!

RAGNELL. Because you broke your word! You don't like punishment. You don't want praise. What do you want? It's you making all the fuss. Everyone else is leaning backwards to excuse you. But no! Not Gawain! You won't accept the judgement of ordinary men. You have to be grand and impossible!

GAWAIN. You're a queer little creature, aren't you?

RAGNELL [*Crossly*]. Be that as it may. Good-bye!

GAWAIN. Where are you off to?

RAGNELL. Back to the Hills, of course. I'll always go back to the Hills. Even if things had gone properly—if I'd stayed here awhile—one night I'd have heard the wind blowing and the horns calling, and followed them home. Now—well, you're running for cover. And so am I.

GAWAIN. Stay here, then.

RAGNELL. Like this?

GAWAIN. You've all been nagging me to face it out. Let's see how brave you are.

RAGNELL. But you can knock people off their horses, if they sneer at you.

GAWAIN. It's not the complete answer. Anyway, I usually fall off myself.

[*Quite unexpectedly, he is overtaken by the erratic laughter of his race.*]

RAGNELL [*Alarmed*]. Gawain! Don't have hysterics!

GAWAIN. I'm just laughing.

RAGNELL. At me?

GAWAIN. No. Generally. Look, if you really want anyone unhorsed, I could try to do it for you.

RAGNELL. You *are* laughing at me! I didn't think you could be cruel.

GAWAIN. I made you a perfectly genuine offer.

RAGNELL. Oh. Oh—I didn't mean to cry here! I only came to say good-bye—and to thank you—for putting a ring on my hand without flinching. And now, you—you offer——! I'm *not* going to cry!

[*But she is crying and he goes over to her.*]

GAWAIN. You'll make your eyes all red and awful.

[*She gives a small wail, somewhere between laughter and weeping.*]

Stop it, you stupid girl! I'm trying to tell you——! If I did stay here—look, you won't have much of a life with me, and that's a fact. I'm just not domesticated. And you'll be flashing back to your Hills at any moment. But—I thought I'd nothing left, and there is one thing. I'm quite handy with a sword. I could protect you. It's not much consolation for what my— what the High Queen did to you—I do wish you'd stop crying! At least she'd not be crowing so much.

[*He puts both arms protectively round* RAGNELL.

[111]

> *For a moment they stay so, like a pair of lost children.*]

It'll be an awful job to face people, but forbye it can be done.

> [*He takes her ugly head in his hands, and kisses her gently, as though she is indeed a child. She steps back, and he is holding a mask. He looks from this to the pale face of the girl. He considers her thoughtfully for a moment.*]

You're quite pretty, really.

RAGNELL. No. I was always rather plain. It's the contrast you notice.

GAWAIN. Och, now it's you can crow! Will I call your brother in, to take a look at you?

RAGNELL. Can you face him, now?

GAWAIN. May as well start with him.

> [*He goes towards the door.*]

RAGNELL. Wait! It isn't quite ended yet. No one else will see me like this—but as the Loathly Lady still.

GAWAIN. Why so?

RAGNELL. Because you have a decision to make. If you see me as I am now, to the rest of the world I'll be loathly. If they see this, to you I'll be hideous. Which will you choose?

GAWAIN. On the whole I prefer you this way.

RAGNELL. So I must show that other face to everyone else. Oh, you've found your courage again—couldn't you stretch it far enough to take my ugliness for your eyes alone. And so let me face the world without shame!

> [*He thinks this over. Having regained most of his usual spirits, he does not really care much, one way or the other. At last he says cheerfully:*]

GAWAIN. You make the decision. I'll be ruled by you.

[*She gives a peal of delighted laughter. She runs
to him, and throws her arms round him, taking
him by surprise.*]

RAGNELL. That's it! That's it! You said it! The spell is
smashed to pieces. Oh, you are a darling! I'll love you
forever, even when I leave you.

GAWAIN. Fine. We can be friends even if we *are* married.
[*She laughs again, and runs to open the door.
She finds the* KING *waiting patiently outside.*]

KING. How are you getting on, my dear?

RAGNELL. Come and see.
[*He enters, looking from her face to that of*
GAWAIN.]

KING. I see a change for the better.
[KYNAN *enters, and* RAGNELL *casts herself into
his arms. The* QUEEN *comes in with* KAY, *and*
GAHERIS *follows them.*]

KYNAN [*Looking at his sister*]. So far, so good. How does
Orkney see you?

RAGNELL. Not loathly, my brother! He said it all, bless
him.

KYNAN. What pushed him over the jump at last? Pity?

RAGNELL. Not he! He started to laugh.

KYNAN. I never thought of that.
[*He turns to the* KING.]
Sir, the time has come to answer the riddle. Only five
seconds of your year are left.

KING. I don't know the answer. I keep saying so.
[RAGNELL *runs and whispers to him. He looks
slightly blank for a moment. Then he laughs.*]
Oh, well—yes. Someone should have thought of that.
The ladies I questioned were not being honest.

KYNAN. Time is over and the sword is gone.

[*Everyone looks at the bare wall where it was hanging.*]

Quickly, before it goes beyond recall! What does a woman most desire in all the world?

KING. Mastery over men.

KYNAN. Exactly.

KING. And the sword? Oh—I've got it.

[*And he has. The sword is belted round his waist. He looks at* KYNAN.]

Well! Perhaps, at last, I may offer you supper?

KYNAN. Sir, I thank you, but my lady will be expecting me home in an hour.

KING. In Northumberland?

KYNAN. The road to the Eildon Hills is the Low Road, and a straight one. For Northumberland, use the word "elsewhere". That is where I go.

[*He bows to the* KING, *then goes to* GAWAIN *and offers his hand.* GAWAIN *hesitates, catches the* KING'S *eye, and takes the hand.* KYNAN *goes to the door, which* GAHERIS *opens for him, and turns there.*]

From one kingdom to another—farewell.

KING. In peace, Kynan.

[*Mist blows across the doorway, and* KYNAN *vanishes into it. A far horn blows.* RAGNELL *turns to* GAWAIN, *and he looks at her disapprovingly.*]

GAWAIN. Mastery over men?

RAGNELL. You gave the answer yourself, when you gave me my own way. If you hadn't, I could not have told the king. You said you'd be ruled by me.

GAWAIN. I was not myself.

[*A thin whistling comes from one of the wine-*

[114]

cups on the table. But only GAHERIS *hears it.*]
If you think I——

GAHERIS. Gawain! It's mother!

GAWAIN. Ach, deamhan [*dyovan*]! Where?

GAHERIS. The wine-cup, there. Whistling!

> [*The whistle sounds again, louder. This time*
> RAGNELL *hears it, too.*]

GAWAIN. I can hear nothing at all.

GAHERIS. Ah, now it's fading. Going right away——

RAGNELL. No, it isn't. Let me speak to her!

> [*She darts to the table, picks up the whistling*
> *cup, and speaks with happy triumph.*]

Madam Morgawse? Gawain is beyond your reach. He
didn't hear you. Your hold on him is broken! We've
beaten you. Not by the death of your son, or his dishonour, but in gaining him his freedom. It's I who hold
him now. This is Ragnell, sister to Kynan of the Eildon
Hills, and in my own shape—wife of Gawain of
Orkney!

> [*There is a thin yell from the cup.* RAGNELL *pours*
> *some wine into it from a flagon. The cry dies*
> *away in a gurgle. The* KING *takes* GAWAIN *down*
> *right, while* RAGNELL *laughs gleefully.*]

Now we're all free of her!

QUEEN. Ragnell, dear——!

> [RAGNELL *goes enquiringly to her. While they*
> *speak together, the* KING *says quietly to his*
> *nephew:*]

KING. There's trouble down at Anderida. Lavain has sent
for help. All the men below are arming now, to ride off
at once. Take my sword for your authority, and lead
them. They'll be glad of you—and all wearing your
green ribbon to show. it.

III. iii

[KAY, *who is standing near, begins to grin to him-self. But* RAGNELL *is still talking to the* QUEEN, *and hears none of this.*]

GAWAIN. Arthur——

[*He gives up, takes the sword, and hugs the* KING *briefly.*]

KING. Don't wait to change your clothes.

GAWAIN. I wasn't going to. Gaheris—we're away!

[*He grabs his brother, and they go off quickly together. The* KING *begins to toy idly with the chess-men on the table.*]

RAGNELL. Well, I just forgot he was there, madam, and that's the truth.

[*She turns to the others.*]

Gawain, did you—? Oh, where is he?

KING. I've sent him into battle, my dear. Three hundred miles away. He's one of my men, you know. Under *my* command. Kay, will you play another game with me?

KAY. Another walk-over!

[*He joins the* KING *at the table, and they sit down, and start setting out the chess-men.* RAGNELL *goes towards the* QUEEN.]

RAGNELL. Just what did I do wrong?

QUEEN. Showed your hand, much too soon after that betraying riddle. Displayed the trap, to a very wary creature. And old clever there let him loose, before he clawed his way out! Men have an answer, too. Instant flight.

RAGNELL [*Lightly*]. I hope he comes back sometime.

QUEEN. Anything is possible, with that one. Heaven knows I'm the last person to advise you, but——

[RAGNELL *goes and sits at her feet, and the* QUEEN *talks to her in an undertone. The* KING *moves a chess-man.*]

KING. Queen's pawn forward.

KAY. A new gambit, eh? It won't win.

KING. Give it a chance, man! Heaven knows I'm not clever at these games, but——

> [*He looks across at the* QUEEN, *and catches her eye. They smile at one another.*]

THE END